DON'T

Give Up!

ACKNOWLEDGING THE STRUGGLE

CELEBRATING RESILIENCE

Revised Edition

DON'T

Give Up!

ACKNOWLEDGING THE STRUGGLE
CELEBRATING RESILIENCE

by

Yedidah Spann

Revised Edition

DEDICATION

This book is dedicated to my Heavenly Father God and to my family and friends!

To my beautiful, enthusiastic, and creative daughter. You are my Precious Diamond and I love you more than words can say! Always shine and never apologize for being the wonderful person God has created you to be. Shine baby shine!

Table of Contents

DEDICATION ....**iv**

Table of Contents ....*v*

INTRODUCTION ....**vii**

CHAPTER 1 1

Celebrate Your Snapback... 1

CHAPTER 2 5

Deliberate Titles... 5

CHAPTER 3 11

Duped 11

CHAPTER 4 23

Butterfly Wings.. 23

CHAPTER 5 34

ARE YOU IN THE CLEAR?... 34

CHAPTER 6 46

I CAN'T SWIM 46

CHAPTER 7 52

SWEETNESS AND GRANDMA WISDOM 52

CHAPTER 8 61

DOES FOSTER CARE?.. 61

CHAPTER 9 66

GOD DOESN'T THROW AWAY BROKEN THINGS 66

CHAPTER 10 ....**72**

GOD WHO WALKS IN THE GARDEN 72

CHAPTER 11 ....**77**

A DIFFERENT KIND OF PASSION 77

CHAPTER 12 ....**81**

HELP ME I'VE FALLEN 81

CHAPTER 13 ....**91**

BETWEEN HERE AND THERE 91

CHAPTER 14 ....**99**

THE RESILIENT 99

Don't Give Up! 108

INTRODUCTION

Imperfectly perfected! Yes that is the phrase! (I guess it is a concept for this book.) From cover to cover, I see this theme being repeated, imperfectly perfected, yet moving forward!

Tonight, I thought I had the perfect cover. Then, as I slept, the current cover of this book came to mind. Excitedly, I jumped up and started flipping back and forth between my two cover choices.

One cover was practically perfect, while the one I knew I needed to choose was not quite what I envisioned. "Why," you ask? I wanted butterflies which were visually appealing with soft, rounded edges and beautiful colors.

My optimal color choice was violet with soft hues of mauve and off white. As I continued to compare both covers, I chuckled to myself.

Ahh; I get it. It's not supposed to be perfect. I finally realized that the front cover was a representation of people who were imperfectly perfected.

Some of the butterflies did not appear as the others, but should they not be recognized? Have you ever heard someone say, "I wish you could change this or that about you?"

Let me share this—inner beauty is not superficial. Instead, it can be found in someone's character in traits such as honesty, compassion, empathy and bravery.

As I look at the cover now, I see butterflies, some not fully developed, some flying sideways, and others appearing to be spiraling downward. There are some which don't look like butterflies at all, yet they are in the overall scheme. Should they be disqualified because they appear to be different? Little ones and big ones in various shapes, colors, and sizes, flying in different directions, but nonetheless flying.

Life is like that, and sometimes, as we journey on this path of life, we find ourselves trying to find ourselves. There is no blueprint, but simply a will to survive and thrive.

Sometimes, we lose our way and find ourselves distracted and diverting from our purpose. Other times we encounter strong currents and winds which cause our frame to feel compromised under intense pressure and situations which make us feel as though we may never rise again. I discovered that the easiest way to fly is with the lightest load.

Lightening the load for me sometimes resembled letting go of my past. It resembled learning the importance of forgiveness. It was in laying down the things I was never meant to carry that I found peace. I had to accept I have a loving Heavenly Father who is always with me. I had to accept I was and am victorious despite what I have been through. His love for me caused me to rise above deep waters of intense pain, tribulation and affliction.

I found out I did not have to fly alone or bear the weight of my own burdens. So I learned how to cast my cares on God, knowing He cares for me as written in First Peter 5:7 (NLT).

This is the reason for writing this book, to let other "butterflies" (people) know it is okay to fly even with broken and imperfect wings. Even if we fall or struggle to break out of the chrysalis once made to protect us, we must press forward and spread our wings.

Sometimes butterflies fly alone, but nonetheless, they fly. I wonder if butterflies know how much they affect their surroundings and add beauty to the atmosphere. Perhaps they don't.

I pray you realize you, like the butterfly, have purpose. Even if your struggle seems great now, please remember these moments are temporary.

Yes, at times there may be negative forces which want you to give up, but there are a great multitude of others, including me who are celebrating you right where you are, even if it is not where you want to be. There is a future ahead of you, so go on and reach for it.

Please remember life is a process. Our Heavenly Father sees your tears and hears your cry. You, my friend, were born to fly. So don't give up!

Note: This book combines my personal experiences with fiction. I will use humor to lessen the emotional effect in some of the stories, as I know laughter in the right context can help lighten feelings associated with trauma. No part of this book is intended to bring shame or judgment, but instead to let you know you are not alone and someone else has walked a similar road. Here's to a better tomorrow. Press on!

CHAPTER 1

Celebrate Your Snapback

OKAY, IT'S TIME. "Time for what?" you ask. Time to celebrate your existence, your resilience, and your "Snapback!"

If I were allowed to add a word to the dictionary this would be my contribution—"Snapbacktivity." It just has a nice ring to it.

As you and I go on this journey through the pages of this book, pages filled with circumstances and situations, tears and triumphs, momentary victims and conquerors—I pray you will be encouraged, as you find hope and strength.

Maybe you have not encountered all or any of the experiences which take place on these pages yet, I still hope you find a way to celebrate and know you are stronger, braver and more resilient than you can imagine.

Yes, you, my friend, have "Snapback!"

"How do you know this?" you ask. I know this, because in spite of all the difficulties, rejections, heartaches, illnesses, grief, and let downs you have encountered, you are still living, still pressing, and still making it happen.

Never stop believing things will get better. Truthfully, unfortunate circumstances have a way of momentarily casting a dark cloud over the essence of our horizons, while threatening our peace and blocking our view.

But, do not despair, for God sees your tears, knows your voice, and He loves you.

As you seek Him, His presence is closer than you can imagine. My aim is to help you realize your pain is real, but it does not define you.

Far too often, I have watched people struggle through tragedies while apologizing for expressing tears and heartfelt emotions. Others have put on masks which cause them to look as if all is well on the outside, yet deep inside they are screaming, "See me! Look at me! Hear me and know me for who I am – not for who you want me to be!"

Not by the color of my skin, the shape of my thighs, hips, lips or educational stance. Not by the size of my bank account, whether it be great or small. And not by the assumptions, rumors, and misnomers given by others which attack the essence of my character.

Instead, accept me for me, for truthfully, me is all God created me to be. Rest assured if you can allow yourself the freedom to accept your emotions—whatever they may be—as part of your humanity, and not as a sign of weakness, you will be well on your way towards hope and healing.

Yes, there is a cry which resonates in the heart of the broken and misunderstood. The cry is oftentimes the same regardless of who expresses it whether male or female, rich or not, educated or not as educated. It is a cry which resides deep in the crevices of a space called "Misunderstood."

So, to you I write, hoping if but for a moment, you and I can focus not primarily on the storm, but on the God who shelters, walks with us and gives us hope and strength in the midst of the storm.

He heals the brokenhearted and binds up their wounds. (Psalm 147:3)

No, despite all these things, overwhelming victory is ours through Christ, who loved us. (Romans 8:37)

Are you broken-hearted? Have you been longing for someone to encourage you and let you know things will get better? Have you cried until you felt you could cry no more?

May you be comforted by the words found in (Psalms 30:5) For his anger lasts only a moment, but his favor lasts a lifetime; weeping may last through the night, but joy comes in the morning.

Has your night season lasted for more than twenty-four hours and you feel you have had enough? There is good news—God mends the hearts of those who are broken and He gives joy to those who have walked in sorrow.

He causes the feet of those who have mourned and persevered through suffering to dance. He lets us know our tears, disappointment, and uncomfortable moments can be used for His glory, and it will work for our good. (Romans *8:28*)

Take courage. God has not forgotten you.

#youcandothis...   #itsnotover...   #itstimestoturnthepage

#dontgiveup

Come on. Let's keep going!

*My definition of Snapback is having the ability to recover after experiencing difficult circumstances or challenges; snapbacktivity; snapbacktuity; snapbackativity.

CHAPTER 2

Deliberate Titles

I REMEMBER WHEN THIS book was nothing more than a passing thought on the road of contemplation, procrastination and possibility. As I reflected on the title, I thought to myself... "Don't Give Up!" "Don't Give Up???

Really Miss Spann? Could you not have thought of a more intriguing title—perhaps something like "Determined Eagles Soar, While Ravenous Lions Bravely Roar?" Okay, maybe not that title. But as I pondered the many tragedies and discouragement people encounter on a daily basis I resolved - "Don't Give Up" was the best option.

But don't give up on what? Don't give on your dreams, your hope, your future, your gifts and talents.

Don't give up on your ability to trust and believe things will get better despite the obstacles you may be facing right now.

Don't give up on your child-like faith which causes you to trust in the ability of a sovereign and unseen God, a Heavenly Father who sees, knows, and loves you.

Don't give up on believing things can and will get better, even if they seem to be getting worse. Don't give up on hoping one day someone will see the beauty which lies within you and treat you with the respect and dignity you deserve.

Don't give up on praying. Don't give up on loving. Don't give up on hoping or on searching for answers even when it seems there are none in sight.

Don't give up in trusting—even when life does not make sense.

Don't give up on your relationship with the Almighty God, and if you have not encountered the blessing of knowing his Son, Jesus Christ as a Savior, Redeemer, and cleanser of sins, don't give up on believing one day you will.

Yes, I was deliberate about the title because I wanted to convey an urgent and heartfelt message, which would not only cause emotions to be stirred, but cause God-given relationships, dreams and purposes to awaken. You know the ones which have been silenced for far too long.

I wanted the grief-stricken, broken, and rejected to find a way to forge ahead and realize there is still a reason to live.

So with this, I ask a question. Where are you in this journey called life?

What negative deliberate titles, if any, have you willingly and maybe unknowingly accepted which are not yours to own?

Titles which someone else may have deliberately placed on you to either bless or attempt to curse you, to raise you up or tear you down, to push you forward or to stifle your progress and discredit your existence.

If you have been crushed by the harsh titles which have been placed on you, I am concerned about how these titles may have affected you. I know all too well how accepting the wrong title can shape one's life in ways that are sometimes not conducive for growth or love.

Accepting the wrong title, particularly if it is negative can deplete you of your energy and place you in a sea of despondency.

Have you accepted a title which does not belong to you? Be careful, because accepting the wrong title or name which was not created for you can cause you to question yourself and make you settle for less than what God has to offer.

Have you found yourself in a space of criticism, finding fault with yourself and others? Are your emotions crushed by a failed relationship or relationships? Have you experienced the betrayal of friendly enemies or found yourself running out of strength as you attempt to rise above waters of rejection and loss?

If so, I write to you and pray your struggles will not subdue your optimism, stifle your praise, or quiet your voice permanently.

If your ministry and message has been silenced, I pray you find it again, proclaim His Word, and use it even if it cracks from years of being suppressed.

The experience of losing does not make us Losers; failing does not make us Failures; and being naïve does not make us stupid.

Those are titles which were never made for us to own. Thankfully, we can renounce and no longer accept them. It may take practice but as we reflect and accept God's Word for our lives, it will become easier. For knowing who and whose we are can alter our outlook on life and change how we feel about ourselves and others.

Practicing positive affirmations from the Word of God can help bring forth a new way of thinking. It may help to post scripture along with quotes in your favorite places. Speak it, write it and accept the good things God says about you. There are many. Allow Holy Spirit to guide you into all truth. The truth defeats any lies which the enemy may be using as a ploy to cause you to give up. Whispers in your ear and attacks from the enemy cannot stand against the truth of God's Word. Use it!

Are there any titles which you have accepted and need to refuse or deliberately change towards yourself or those you love?

Make a daily practice of verbalizing the titles which the Almighty God has spoken about you. Titles which speak of His love toward you and His promises for your life.

Practice speaking these promises and titles until you not only hear them, but until you accept and replace them above the negative labels which may have been engrained in the tapestry of your mind, heart, and spirit. Practice may not make perfect, but it does make better. Now is a very good time to start.

Let's start today while saying, *I am not a failure. I am God's handiwork. I am created for good things and a good work. I am blessed and highly favored. I am above only and not beneath. I am the head and not the tail. I am worthy of God's love and favor. I am a portal of God's peace. I am loved.*

Try saying the aforementioned affirmations every day, even if you don't believe them at first. Renounce and denounce the lies of the enemy and proclaim God's word over your heart mind and spirit.

Please don't wait for others to cheer you on. Start to speak into your own life!

First Samuel 30:6 (NLT) reads, "... but David encouraged himself in the Lord."

Here are a few scriptures to ponder which can help with replacing negative thoughts.

"I knew you before you were in your mother's womb. Before you were born I set you apart and appointed you as my prophet to the nations." (Jeremiah 1:5, NLT)

"But you are not like that, for you are a chosen people. You are royal priests, a holy nation. God's very own possession. As a result, you can show others the goodness of God, for he called you out of the darkness into his wonderful light." (1 Peter 2:9, NLT)

"See how very much our Father loves us, for He calls us his children, and that is what we are! But the people who belong to this world don't recognize that we are God's children because they don't know him.

2Dear friends, we are already God's children, but He has not yet shown us what we will be like when Christ appears. But we do know that we will be like him, for we will see him as he really is." (John 3:1-2, NLT)

"God is our refuge and strength, always ready to help in times of trouble.2So we will not fear when earthquakes come and the mountains crumble into the sea..." (Psalm 46:1, NLT)

Heavenly Father, today, I acknowledge according to your Word, I am victorious, I am strong, I am resilient and I am more than a

Conqueror. Help me to let go of the negative titles which have stunted my growth spiritually, mentally and physically.

I renounce fear, failure and rejection and proclaim faith, victory and acceptance by those who truly love you.

I speak that I can have life and that I am not a failure. Instead, I am blessed by You and I am loved, because you love me more than I could ever imagine.

I believe and receive you have spoken good things concerning me and I will receive them by faith. In your great and mighty name I pray. Amen.

Let's go a little further...

CHAPTER 3

Duped

She held him closely, until it seemed their bodies became one. She could feel the warmth of his breath, moving in and out and out and in on her cheeks. He was leaving again.

Despite all of the harsh words he would say from time to time, she truly loved him and wanted him to stay.

"Do you really have to leave?" she asked.

He lovingly bent down to kiss her as she tippy toed to return the favor. Then, without a word he swiftly turned, grabbed his luggage, walked to the door and without looking back closed the door behind him.

There she stood, overcome with overwhelming emotions. She wondered if there were anything she could have done to make him stay.

The urge to sob, to scream, to chase after him, grew stronger and stronger with each passing moment. She could barely breathe and felt as if she was suffocating with each inhale and exhale.

"How am I going to live without him for such a long period of time?" she thought.

She always considered herself to be strong like iron, but the thought of being away from him as he worked on a project out of state (and possibly country) left her feeling incomplete and vulnerable.

"I love you baby," she said softly. Yet, he was already gone. Truthfully, he had been gone for some time; she just tried to deny it.

Her intense and unselfish love for him and what seemed perfect overshadowed the lie which was before her.

"He does love me. Doesn't he?" This was a question she pondered constantly; it was the inner wrestling she encountered on a daily basis. Her love for him made what some referred to as common sense seem very uncommon.

As she walked into the kitchen the weight of emotions she experienced overtook her as she grabbed the refrigerator while slowly crumbling to the floor. By now she was sobbing intensely.

Suddenly the words she penned to a song many years before, started to ring in her mind;

Tears falling from my face,
Since the day you broke my heart
I did not recognize
We wouldn't be getting together
We'd only stay apart

Alone, she continued weeping while holding her abdomen, gasping with every wave of emotion. Although she could not put her finger on it she sensed something was terribly wrong... then a flutter and soft kick from within, a reminder she was not alone.

"Yes, baby girl," she said, wiping away the tears which were gushing from her eyes and trickling down the sides of her chin. "Mommy will be strong while daddy is gone."

That day Patience Jackson questioned the undeniable and overwhelming sense of loneliness and grief she felt.

She wanted to be strong, but found it difficult as she wondered, if her "Husband," would be back in time for the birth of their unborn child?

He was leaving for an assignment, again, which would probably not allow him to speak with her for weeks.

At first he told her he did not want her to work, which she found to be quite difficult. She was an independent woman who thrived on being a go-getter and making things happen, yet she wanted to be a good wife and reluctantly consented to his request. After a short period of time he found himself in financial straits and allowed her to work until his situation "cleared up."

At first, his calls were relatively frequent, but as days moved on, his calls became fewer and fewer while her need to hear his voice and be comforted became greater and greater.

As she held her phone in her hand she scrolled through his text messages like someone in need of a fix. His sweet words comforted her extreme longing.

"My beautiful darling, I am nothing without you, the Heavens answered my prayers when I lay eyes on you. I am a blessed man because of you. Thank you for choosing me, my Queen."

His messages were so poetic and, for moments on end, soothed her deep longing.

Oh, how she wanted to nestle in his big strong arms and hear the rhythmic beating of his heart as she lay her head on his chest. "Things will get better," she thought.

His written words momentarily filled the gap of emptiness and distance between them. She oftentimes wondered how he could write such poetic phrases when they were apart, but would sometimes use harsh words when they were together.

"Our daughter has an angel for a mother, and I am blessed with a beautiful Queen for a wife." Originally his writings truly soothed her anxieties until the communication completely stopped.

During those lonely moments when he was unable to call she would reach for old greeting cards and trace his salutation with her finger.

"To my darling wife." Just hearing those words made her feel secure and loved. Later she would sleep with his letters, holding them close to her heart, longing, hoping, and praying.

She wondered if he were safe and desperately needed to hear his voice.

"Come on girl, you've got this, be strong," she thought, as she continued to reason beyond hope and hope beyond reason still wrestling with the inevitable. She wondered why she was unable to reach him on his phone. I hope he is okay, she thought.

This was a very cold winter season in Patience Jackson's life. She found herself trying to protect herself from the harsh, cold blow of words which came from those who she expected to comfort her.

She had encouraged others during their times of affliction and sorrow. Surely she would receive the same—so she thought. Yet, this was not the case.

The ridicule, resentment, judgment and rejection she encountered made her already difficult situation seem unbearable.

Days turned into months, months into years, and still no word from her love who she referred to as her "Knight in Armor."

She found herself praying for the night and hoping for the day. But when the day came she only wanted to shut out the light, close the blinds and pull the covers over her head. This was her night season.

Constantly she walked the floor at night unable to sleep, wondering if even God had forgotten about her.

However, the need to care for her child superseded her brokenness and kept her going despite thoughts which chided without mercy, urging her to give up and end it all. "Don't give up!" she wrote on a yellow piece of paper in purple ink and taped it on the mirror.

"I gave my vows—for better or for worse, for richer or poorer." "This is the worse," she thought, "It has to get better from here!"

Little did she know it was going to get worse, much worse.

After a number of grueling months of waiting, the phone rang. Surely it was Sonny. Her loneliness and longing would finally be satisfied. Hoping this wasn't another prank phone call, she picked up the phone. She was filled with so much excitement, she could barely breathe. The anticipation was too great.

However, much to her regret and surprise, it was not the voice of her "husband," but another voice, an unkind voice telling her of infidelity, gifts, children and a marriage prior to her meeting him.

"It can't be," she thought. "He told me he was a virgin and that he had never been married before."

She was not his first as she had been led to believe. She had given him the gift of money and her virginity, something she had reserved well into her thirties... and now this.

Once again, her knees buckled beneath her. She could not tell if it was the weight of the news or of her own disbelief which caused the thoughts in her head to swim like an ocean of wild Piranha quickly chewing and ripping away at her dreams of being a good wife and having a beautiful family.

For better or ...for worse! How could she not have known? Why didn't she see the signs? She had given her time, her love, her finances and her passion only to find she had been fooled, tricked, and hoodwinked. Yes, she had been duped.

Have you ever been duped?

If you have, I am sure you were devastated. This magnitude of love betrayal can be synonymous with that of a prized fighter getting caught off guard and being knocked out from a one two punch.

Just like that in an instant one phone call, one visit, one unexpected finding or encounter on social media can change your whole perspective from that of ecstasy to agony.

Being duped or tricked can break down the strongest of men and cause the savviest of women to cower in fear like a little girl. A life of positivity, romance, and ecstasy can quickly turn into disbelief and uncertainty when the truth comes out.

Sweet nothings suddenly become empty promises and life can seem like nothing more than sandcastles crumbling in the sky; what once resembled a relationship of near perfection with fluffy clouds becomes just plain old storm clouds.

One moment you are there in the sun, and then, bam, just like that —hey who turned off the lights?

Perhaps you know of someone who has been duped, but then again, perhaps you do not. Truthfully, many persons who experience this level of betrayal, often suffer in silence too ashamed to tell, too embarrassed to hear the reactions of friends and family and too shocked to even accept it themselves. The Silent Sufferers.

Somehow the enemy of their soul caused them to feel as if no one understood, cared or had experienced the same thing. So they resorted to facing their pain alone. I wish they knew God saw. I wish they knew how beautiful and how priceless they are, despite the pain.

The other day I read an article of a well-known actress who shared her story of love betrayal. Imagine the strength she had to muster up in order to find the courage to push past her own feelings and share her story with the world.

Truth is, we often find healing as we share our stories with others.

Sharing with the right person brings us out of hiding and with the help of the Lord delivers us from shame, fear, and maybe even condemnation.

Can you imagine the countless men and women who were able to identify with this well-known actress?

Oftentimes sharing can become liberating not just for those who share, but also for those who may be too embarrassed to tell. When you have been betrayed it is important to receive real and true love to overshadow the deception and lies which may come to stifle your future.

"And you will know the truth, and the truth will set you free." - John 8:32

Lies make us feel depleted, rejected and ashamed, yet truth brings us life and hope. Lies distract us from the wonderful promises of God and cause us to oftentimes step away from what God has called us to due to shame and embarrassment.

Psalm 137:1 speaks of a time when the children of Israel were faced with great discouragement and as a consequence found themselves putting down their instruments and not singing their song of victory.

It reads on this wise, "Beside the rivers of Babylon, here we sat down, yea, we wept when we remembered Zion." - Psalm 137:1.

In this particular passage the children of Israel were held captive by their enemy.

As they reminisced and thought about previous days when they were in a better place, they found themselves feeling utterly discouraged, as their current status did not equate to the moments of joy they felt when they were in a different place.

They remembered their time of celebrating and wondered how could they even sing in this strange place while surrounded by their enemies? Their song was not really gone, they were just not able to find the strength to sing in their temporary and hopeless state.

Truthfully, they saw no resolution in sight. It's a wrap. Let's just hang our harps on the willow tree and forget about it. *Don't do it!*

I can remember a number of times when I was hopeless and found it difficult to sing. As a matter of fact, it hurt to even think about uttering a tune. It pained me both mentally and even physically.

These were moments when I experienced betrayal, rejection and even grief. It was as if I was caught up in an emotional blizzard that went on for years.

My heart was broken and I was confused wondering how and why people I loved had decided to assassinate my character while on the other hand smiling and telling me they loved me.

I wondered what made me keep falling in love with men who celebrated me behind closed doors, but humiliated me in public. Men who had a motive which I knew nothing about.

I thought people who told you they loved you really meant it. Was there no reverence for the God we both claimed to serve? I made a mistake. I thought I was loved, but I was wrong. It truly broke my heart in places I did not know existed.

The realization was time and time again I was drifting further and further away from my ONE TRUE LOVE—my Lord and Savior Jesus Christ!

As I sought the Lord in prayer, I discovered in some instances God was giving me warnings in the form of dreams, but I found it hard to wake up. I was in denial. I was being betrayed and my Heavenly Father knew it even though I did not.

I can remember the dreams which were so vivid I could not ignore them. In one dream I was talking to a young man and there was no connection to the other end of the phone line.

In another dream someone gave me an engagement ring with a black web over it. Don't get me wrong, these men may have been right for someone, but God as a loving Father was showing me they were not right for me. There was truly no connection.

Mostly, I found myself stepping back from where I knew God was calling me to. The more time I poured into empty relationships (which were not ordained by God), the more I found myself heartbroken. I discovered if a person only celebrated me behind closed doors and then acted totally different when we were in front of people, there was a reason for that and I needed to pay attention to that very obvious sign.

Honestly, it was difficult to take notice when I was allowing my heart to lead instead of wisdom. Anytime I allowed someone to fill the space where God did not intend for them to be was always trouble. I discovered placing someone in a space reserved for God was a form of idolatry. Yikes! No one else was to be my optimal source of encouragement.

No one else was supposed to be able to rob me of my joy, my peace or my purpose. That's just too much power.

I recognized no one had loved me as much as the Lord and attempting to put someone in His place would never work. So I repented.

Anytime I found myself feeling depleted, depressed, or even confused, that was a red flag. Yet, there was a part of me causing me to feel as if it were my fault, that I should not pay attention to how I was being treated. I mean, I was the kind of person who used to place others people's feelings before my own, even if they were stepping on my emotions and making me feel foolish.

My mother once told me, "You are not "Florence Nightingale!" Wait who?

She kept trying to tell me I could not fix a man, or anyone for that matter. They had to be willing to fix themselves or at least allow God to do it. I honestly thought I was helping them, but I was not. I was enabling them to continue in harmful and deceitful behavior which was unhealthy.

So, there I was broken-hearted, perplexed, and alone.

How could I sing knowing I had not only let God down but also myself and those who expected me to succeed?

I now know I should have continued to sing in public more, even if I sounded like a broken-winged sparrow.

I finally discovered there was strength in my song. There was comfort and healing not only in the words, but in the worship—a melody which I released to God as sweet perfume and the offering of my affection which belonged to Him and Him alone. While I was singing there were others who stated they were being healed as well.

So, I urge you, even in discouragement don't put down your instrument, don't stifle your song or downplay your dance. As a matter of fact, I think those are the times when we should sing and praise even harder and worship God with all of our being.

It is true we will experience deep, uncomfortable moments where the joy we once felt seems unobtainable. But does this mean God has left the building?

Does this mean, He is a God who rejoices with those who are doing well and abandons the broken and faint of heart? Absolutely not! As a matter of fact, He is the only One I know who loves unconditionally!

Our Father never abandons us! Neither does He give up on us when He sees we are really trying. His love is patient, kind, and immeasurable and if you have been duped I want you to receive you will make it through this. I want you to realize you are worth being loved.

Some may call you negative names, some may even call you gullible, crazy or stupid, but I say you are beautiful, (handsome if a man) and you have a loving and caring heart.

A heart which is so precious, a heart you need to protect for the love God has ordained for your life. He is out there. She is out there. Be patient and allow God to heal your deep rooted wounds. Believe it or not you will be able to release the love which you may have stifled for fear of being hurt again. Some may choose to walk alone, but I pray you make that choice in freedom.

You may need to go for pastoral counseling or therapy along with praying and changing your thoughts and actions. For me forgiveness was super important (as it will be for you).

I had to realize human beings can only be human and take the focus off of the person and situation and place it on God, while believing there was still hope for my life.

Be kind to yourself. Be mindful of what you watch, who you confide in, and who you are listening to. Everyone cannot understand the pain you have experienced and that's okay too. It's time for you to be healed in Jesus' name.

Father I pray for the duped, the deceived, the used and abused. You know the lies they have been told, even about themselves.

I pray Father, You deliver them from the torment of the past and let them know they were created mainly to love and worship You. I pray the person reading this accepts they no longer need to resort to feelings of helplessness and hopelessness but that they start to have a positive outlook on life despite all they have been through.

I pray they are no longer consumed with feelings of embarrassment or shame. I pray they realize they never have to be people-pleasers.

I pray they give you every tear, every broken dream, every feeling of abandonment and rejection.

I pray they forgive those who have lied on them and made them to look bad so that they could look good. I pray for the Spirit of comfort and healing, the Holy Spirit, to come upon them as they learn the importance of forgiving those who have wronged them, used and maybe even abused them.

I pray they learn to release the pain to you instead of trying to handle it on their own. You know Lord. You see and You care.

May they no longer look at themselves as being anything but your child and may they celebrate in knowing you know the end from the beginning and that they never need to settle for less! Amen!

Here is to your new day, my friend. Don't you dare give up!

CHAPTER 4

Butterfly Wings

Little caterpillar
- Inching slowly along the ground- I wonder if you know
One day you will fly
Effortlessly,
Beautifully,
Carefully,
Without restriction.
Flutter, flutter, through the air. No more below or beneath.
No longer frowned on, poked at
Or looked at in disgust.
Go through, little caterpillar... Your process will one day change
your name.

If you are reading this page, there is a strong possibility you are in the midst of, or have experienced a time in your life, where you felt like throwing in the towel, forgetting about everything, and just plain old giving up.

Truthfully, giving up seems easy when you feel there is no reason to live.

During difficult moments, it is hard to stand, when your legs keep buckling under the weight of intense pressure you are experiencing day in and day out. I write to you to tell you that you have to make it. You have to breathe; you have to live, and you have to survive. "Why?" Because.

I know. What kind of a response is that . . . because? Yet, I have a reason for saying this. We can equate the processes we deal with to the life of a caterpillar turned to butterfly. Please give me a moment to further explain.

You see, I often wondered about the process of caterpillars in comparison to humans. Both start off in one place and transition to another. Both go through stages and both have to press through obstacles and difficulties in order to survive.

To this end, I imagined having a talk with a butterfly who knew a thing or two about life. I imagined myself following the now butterfly, once caterpillar, through a very difficult process which developed into a miraculous occurrence.

The conversation started something like this: "Butterfly?" I asked, "Why do you crawl around on the ground, then wrap yourself up until nothing is showing, and then use all of your strength to break through the very thing you created to protect yourself?

I imagine the butterfly and I going on a journey, far too great for me to understand.

As the butterfly looks at me, it does not say a word and then beckons for me to follow.

Suddenly, the butterfly begins to speak. "I remember when I was a lone caterpillar, inching slowly across the grass. I inched along, minding my own business, and my only goal in life was to reach my destination. The grass was familiar to me, but as I continued along, I felt my frame encounter a hard substance.

The substance was so different from what I was used to, and I wanted to turn back to what was familiar—my soft, green grass. But I continued to inch forward anyway.

Along the way I encountered people, people who called me out my name and said I was "yucky, slimy, gross, and even ugly." I wanted to tell them, "My name is not yucky. I am not ugly. I was created this way by my Maker." But they never bothered to listen and continued ridiculing me, ignoring my very apparent embarrassment. I also encountered people who poked me with sticks and laughed as I writhed fear.

Others lifted me up and dropped me from a distance and chuckled with glee as I plummeted to the ground squirming in severe pain. I wondered if they knew they were breaking me. I wondered if they wanted to destroy me on purpose, because I did not look like them or act like them. But why should I?

I wondered if they even cared about the things which were important to me, including my need to live and fulfill my destiny. Maybe there was no reason for their disregard of my feelings or invasion of space. But they cared nothing of my emotions or my opinion. So, after enjoying their time of abusing me, they would finally laugh again and leave me to suffer alone. Yet, they never left me the way they found me. When they found me, I was whole, but when they left me, I was wounded and broken.

Before they came into my life I was sure of my path, but in this unfamiliar space I was left unsure and confused.

What did I do to receive such treatment? I wondered what would cause someone to prod me and use me for sport without regard. Maybe they were more concerned about themselves, their life, and their ability to do harm to those who appeared vulnerable. Maybe it was entertaining.

I am a caterpillar. I was made this way, born this way. Why would someone hate me for being me when I had no choice in my making? I kept hearing I was going to be beautiful one day and not to look at my current situation. They kept telling me I was created for God's glory and for a purpose, but how could that be? Look at how I have been treated. Look at me!

But for some reason I felt a compelling desire to keep crawling and to keep moving. Towards what? I did not know but I continued on struggling while in pain, slowly, but still pressing forward.

For some reason something deep inside of me tells me it is time. Although I am tired I continue to move on, to find a space where I can be alone and hidden from my fears and unfriendly elements. I continue looking for my perfect hiding spot until— Eureka! I found it! This area underneath this humongous milkweed leaf will certainly keep my enemies out! I must start transitioning into my next stage. I start to shed my skin, the outer part, which was wounded until I reveal my chrysalis.

There I was twisting, turning, and fidgeting, spinning almost out of control. I know that I must do this; it is my reason for living. It is what I am born to do; at least that's what all of the other caterpillars did.

I feel protected, and at peace, I can hear the noise of nature around me, yet I am untouched and I feel safe.

As time progresses however, I also discover that I feel imprisoned by this moment of solace in my self-created encasement and I find myself wrestling with my conception.

Why was I even born? Is it me? Did I do something to deserve this treatment? Is this all I was created to be—a lonely caterpillar?

At first I was comforted to be in this space, yet reality sets in and I realize no one can get in, but neither can I get out.

While reflecting I feel something happening to me which I have never felt before. I am changing. I continue wondering if I picked the right hiding spot, and if this was part of that thing called process. I recognize picking the right place to develop determined my survival. I hoped I had it right and felt doubtful and fearful. I feel alone and I can't talk to anyone and that frustrates me!

It is in this lonely, broken space where I am made to reason, contemplate and accept. Is there a reason for me to live?

Did my Maker create me and forget about me? I am in my most difficult moment, is He even here? Is there a greater purpose for my life?

Do I not see it? Am I valuable, and will I make an impact as a result? Is there anything worth fighting for?

I find myself experiencing feelings of discouragement, perplexity, dismay, and on the other hand, anticipation and exhilaration far greater than anything I could have ever imagined. Expectancy.

Mostly I am beginning not to like this stage at all. My caterpillar family did not warn me about this. I have subjected myself to intense and emotional pain, and I cannot escape from it. These growing pains are excruciating, and I am fearful that I might not make it out of this chrysalis alive. Now, not only am I dealing with the exterior pain of those who could not see my worth, I am also wrestling with my own inner pain and disappointments with myself, my struggles with my weaknesses and flaws.

Things which were bottled up inside of me started to spew out. It was grotesque and uncomfortable. Somehow, I continued.

Somewhere deep inside my being, I found the courage and the strength and the overwhelming need to press through the process.

I was reminded that my Maker knew what I would be long before I was created. I could hear His voice comforting me, saying, "Before I made you in your mother's womb, I knew you…"(Jeremiah 1:5, NLT) and so I succumbed to the process, to the emotional pain, to the hope that one day I will be transformed into who God ultimately created me to be. Honestly, I did not know what that was, yet I pressed anyway.

I resolved My Maker knew what I would become even while I was a caterpillar. He knew He had a plan, even while I was faced with rejection and mistreatment. Long before I entered the chrysalis, He saw me.

So I focused all the more on being alone with my Creator; changing, evolving, breaking, shifting, healing, stretching and becoming.

Yes, I yielded until I reached one of the darkest and most difficult times ever—a time where I perceived I was going to die.

I was devastated and mortified, yet again during this extremely catastrophic intensity, I could hear the tender voice of my Maker saying, Peace be still… Weeping may endure for the night but joy was coming in the morning, (Psalms 30:5) and my faith and hope grew. The Lord will bring me out of this, and I will be a new creature!

Then all of a sudden, out from the darkness, I heard it. It was the voice of power and reason, of comfort and ingenuity, of light and life.

A sovereign majestic voice which carried the strength of mountains and oceans and the beauty and sweet fragrance of a lily.

As He spoke, His aroma filled the air and brightened the atmosphere. He told me to stretch, yet as I tried to move, I felt confined and stuck.

Yet beyond reasoning, I was obedient to His word and continued to stretch, groaning with every move. It was so hard, even harder than when I went in to be hidden and separated from the world. But despite my own rationalizing and will to give up, I continued to heed his command "Live my child. Live!" As I writhed in pain, "Live!" As I wondered why I had to take this route, "Live!"

As I wanted to give up because giving up seemed much easier than pressing through the pain, "Live!"

With every struggle, His voice became stronger as if it was blowing life into what had become desolate. My dreams, my hope of things getting better, were coming to life inside of me.

My will to be and to become better than what I was birthing inside of me. A shift and atmospheric change was enlightening the darkness. Breathe...life...breathe... peace...breathe... ("Breathe, son, breathe." "Breathe, daughter, breathe.")

The light of my Maker, who I now recognized as Heavenly Father, illuminated the atmosphere, so I focused solely on Him as my life depended on it.

I do not know when it happened, but I started to feel a change. Something was different.

After the struggle, I recognized I was no longer the same. Something unrecognizable, something brilliant, and yet unknown, happened to me.

While I was focusing on my Creator in the solitude of my affliction, My Maker was working, shaping and making me new.

I perceived the space I had resorted to and accepted as my continued dwelling place was no longer sufficient for what I had become. I felt as though I would suffocate if I did not try to get out of it. This darkened lonely space which once consoled my aching and discomfort while protecting me from the elements could no longer confine me. Yes, I was changed by the process!

I felt a part of me I have never known before. I pushed this unknown contraption outside of my comfort zone. Whew that was hard work! "What is this?" I thought. My frame was no longer the same. I was bigger than when I first went in.

I felt this thing I had never felt before, and I kept feeling the need to stretch it out. Then I felt another one on the other side. What in the world is happening to me?

I then heard the familiar voice of my Maker calling me out of the darkness into a majestic light and I was excited to oblige. "Don't be afraid. Push!" I heard Him say.

I push, realizing my life depends on it, because it does! I push until I am completely out of my encasement. And I move in a way I have never moved before, I look into a nearby pond and reflected in the water is the most beautiful, brightly colored creature I have ever seen. Then I realize—it is me!

As the rays of the sun irradiated my entire being, fluttering and swirling, dancing and twirling—I celebrate I have been positively changed by the process. Yes, My Maker changed me! This has to be what they refer to as, "beauty for ashes." (Isaiah 61: 3)

I am finally free! I am no longer a lonely caterpillar, to be poked at, rejected or hated. I am no longer an insect writhing on the ground; I am no longer considered grotesque and ugly, as some once called me.

No, I am even more beautiful than ever before. This process has transformed me.

I went in broken, but gained something I never thought obtainable—wings. Wings to fly above the ground.

I then see people looking and pointing at me not as before when I was a caterpillar, they are rejoicing and admiring my new colors. Then I hear my Maker call me "Butterfly!" I dance in the wind. Yes, I am a "Butterfly."

The process has changed my name. I obtained character and color which I would not have gained if I had not submitted to the process.

Not only am I this new me, but others around me are able to see it as well. So I lift my head towards the clouds and I fly."

A New Chapter in Life

If the caterpillar could speak, I wonder what it would say to those who have been broken and prodded, ridiculed and rejected. I am sure it would say keep on going and don't give up.

You may not see it now, but there is a time, when you will fly. The caterpillar did not know it would gain wings; it just knew to keep on moving forward, not just with its body, but moreover with the instinct to survive. It had to defy the odds which were stacked against it, just as we must. It had to press forward until it obtained its wings, wings which could only be formed after experiencing great opposition. These wings exemplified the glory of God obtained from the struggle, wings that grew and stretched because of the innate ability to forge ahead while submitting and accepting the uncomfortable.

So to you my friend, I pray your development brings you to the place where you are able to accept and experience the process, much like the butterfly. If you allow it, inner beauty and strength will be revealed.

May your struggles bring you to where your life is free to display brilliant colors which are birthed through perseverance and reliance in our Heavenly Father.

May you realize your Maker is with you in every chrysalis-like experience. I encourage you to allow yourself the freedom to accept, trust, and hope through the process.

May your faith in God cause you to soar on wings of faith, hope and love as you abound, and transform from mourning to a place of celebration, dancing, and unapologetic living!

I pray your wings continuously "Snapback," after every storm. As we share our stories may we allow ourselves the freedom to release pain and even shame while letting others know they are not alone.

I think we all know someone, including ourselves, who needs somebody, somewhere, sometimes to cheer us on, while shouting, "Don't Give Up!" Is there someone you know who could use a word of encouragement? You may hold the answer, the prayer, or the message. So hang in there.

Keep on pressing until you rise like the butterfly. Keep on fluttering to a place of victory and whatever happens "Don't give up!"

CHAPTER 5

ARE YOU IN THE CLEAR?

When I was younger, I used to enjoy watching medical dramas. I was amazed as I watched scenes of patients rushed to the Emergency Room while doctors and nurses rallied around them in an attempt to quickly diagnose their prognosis and basically save their lives.

"Give me 5ccs of this and 10ccs of that!" Although I was totally intrigued by the show at large, there were heightened moments which sucked me completely into the scene as the plot thickened while an actor or actress lay there motionless.

To say I was captivated was an understatement. I usually scooted to the edge of my seat, while holding my breath unable to even take a bite of whatever I was eating. Oftentimes the situation would escalate, causing the team to go into STAT mode - and then it happened... "Beeeeeeepppppp!!!!" The patient flatlines.

Immediately when I hear this sound, my heart starts racing and my adrenaline increases. I imagine myself becoming an integral part of the team while yelling at the television screen "Come on, come on! Hurry Up!"

You would think they could hear me the way I was carrying on. All I could think was, "Please don't let my brother come in here and turn the channel to watch that darn Kung Fu foolishness!" I am laughing while I am writing this. Those were fun times with my brother.

Yes, this was a dire moment. All of the actors feverishly worked together attempting to resuscitate the motionless victim.

But when their initial efforts failed, they automatically sprang into action and pulled out the big one...the crash cart...the defibrillator!

In an instant, all of the medical staff were instructed to back up, except for one, the Chief in charge. I can recall my heightened level of excitement while wondering what was going to happen next.

"This is it," I thought as I clasped my hands together with excitement.

The Chief would then rub the steel paddles of the defibrillator together, hold them up, and then place them on the lifeless victim, "CLEAR!"

Oftentimes, the patient would not move right away, which downright worried me. I was concerned for the doctor, worried about the victim, and even went as far as to think of what would happen to the family. I just had to help them. I imagined them calling, "Dr. Spann to the rescue!" and with that, I started yelling at the lifeless body on the screen, "Get up! Come on, get up!"

It was fascinating and quite entertaining for me as a teenager to watch this level of drama. Back then it was entertaining, but not so much in real-life. I found that out when my mother passed away. No, that was not any fun at all.

However, back then I additionally enjoyed watching real-life programs which showed people transitioning from life to death and then coming back to life again.

Each story showed a familiar thread as the interviewees recalled their bodies becoming feather-like while being lifted up into the air as they viewed everything that was happening to them below.

Many of them recollected seeing what was taking place in the room and expressed feeling a great sense of peace and euphoria.

One young man even told of having a conversation with Jesus. Those interviews often gave me hope as I thought of my own loved ones who had transitioned from life to death.

Yes, these shows really got to me as I continued to think more and more about the process of bringing someone back to life.

I could not help but to correlate it to real life circumstances. One moment you can have a lot of people around you, supporting and befriending you, and then, in an instant during the most devastating and earth-shattering moments of your life, it is as if someone yells "Clear!" and everyone disperses.

Are you in the clear or ever felt like you were? It is the moment when your finances seem to shrivel up, your health is failing, your marriage and relationships are rockier than, "Mount Everest," and nothing seems to be going the way you expected. It is a time when you find out your loved one has been diagnosed with a debilitating disease or when you hear the news of an unexpected loss.

It is when you hoped and prayed for a situation to change and received totally the opposite. It is a time when your mental stability can be compromised as you try to navigate through the normalcy of everyday life, when nothing is normal anymore. CLEAR!

I have been there more than once, in a space where I felt all hope was gone and someone shut off the light at the end of the tunnel. With eyes wide open I grabbed through the air like someone who had lost not only their physical sight, but also their hope.

During these times I often wondered, "Where is everybody? Why am I constantly left alone during the most critical moments in my life? What did I do to deserve this?"

I would sit and ponder, "Where are all of the people who told me they would be with me through thick and thin? Where are they now?" My family was not included in this as I chose not to tell them about these happenstances.

During those seemingly endless days and sleepless nights, I can recall feeling betrayed, abandoned and helpless. Truthfully, I was downright devastated!

Yet, I now know God used those moments to show me He was a lot like the "Chief in charge," defibrillator in hand, telling everyone in the room to stand clear.

You see, truth be told, when there are too many people around, giving advice, and trying to "fix" your situation(s), confusion can step in and make things worse. God, my Chief, stepped in right on time and told everyone to move out of the way! He's protecting me from dangers seen and unseen as I lie there on the table. As He charges to two-hundred, His perfect love ignites my heart and heals my brokenness until I am changed forever. When all hope was gone, His love and reassurance surged through the broken chambers of my innermost being and commanded me to live when all I knew to do was die.

There is one instance I can remember like yesterday. There I was alone and confused trying to figure out how I was going to live without my mother. It was not enough to have watched her suffer and take her last breath, but now I had to learn how to be a mother without having her instruction and guidance.

Additionally, I had become a single parent although I had no idea this was going to happen. No not me? Yes me. All of my dreams and hopes of having a blessed, strong, God-fearing family were gone in an instant. All I had at this point was a ring without a promise, a title of wife, without a husband.

None of it made sense to me and as reality started to set in I felt as if the world were crumbling all around me. I wanted to know the truth, but when I finally heard the truth, it was almost unbearable. I wondered how something like that could happen to me. Regretfully, I was conned, but I know I am not he only one. So I turned it over to God.

Ever pour your emotions into a space where God never intended it to be? If so, there is healing for your wounded emotions. Nothing is too hard for God.

Back then I discovered there was something called "Street smarts," and if the teacher were looking for a star student in that category, it was not me.

There were many sleepless nights and moments when I wanted to pull the cover over my head and make myself believe it was a bad dream, but then I would hear the sweetest sounds coming from my little one which snapped me back to reality. "I'm a mommy." CLEAR!!!

Who in the world is going to understand what has happened to me? I heard the horrible things people were saying, but wondered why they would not come to me to find out the truth.

The rumors frightened me, because I kept wondering, "How could people come up with such lies and not be afraid they would be struck by lightning?"

This was a very lonely time. All of those incidents took me to a place of homelessness and severe depression. Yes a woman of faith wounded and depressed. At times I found a way to smile on the outside, but deep inside I felt completely messed up. The trauma, the stress, the loneliness. I cried so much when my daughter fell asleep until my throat ached and it was not because I was making a sound. Ever cried silent tears? I felt as though I had let my little one down and wondered why she could not have been born when I was in a better place at a better time in my life.

However God, our Heavenly Father, spoke to my mind which was full of perplexity, confusion and sorrow and as I shared my anguish with Him. My Heavenly Father started the process of reversing my pain. He used strangers to encourage me. Somehow they would find me to let me know the process was not going to kill me because I had a message for the wounded, and God was going to get the glory out of this situation and out of all of the other ones I had encountered by any means necessary.

At first I kept thinking about better days when I was walking around with my briefcase, high heels and fashionable attire in a career I loved. But at that time all of that was gone. I remembered packing our suitcase and thinking I can't pack my clothes; we need hers.

There was no way I could push a carriage and two suitcases, although I tried.

There I was walking with nowhere to go when the skies opened up and a blizzard started. Lord have mercy! Who could I tell? Who would understand?

This was the day I had a choice to make. Either give up or "Don't give up!"

Either chose to go into a shelter, something I thought I would never do, or allow my pride to overtake me. Well that day pride went out the door.

I will never forget that day! I went to find a place to stay and the person requested a very high amount – just for a room.

Yikes! I had given my money away in hopes things would get better, but they got worse. Broken promises and an apartment I enjoyed. All gone. When I arrived at a place called the Path, I looked around and noticed there were so many people there who were struggling as well. I wondered, "Why?"

Men and women who probably thought they would never end up in a situation like that, longing for shelter from the storm. I saw a young woman with a pair of sandals on and thought, "How could I not give her my other pair of boots." So I shared, knowing that is what life and love is about. Sharing and encouraging even when you feel you have very little or nothing to give. Sometimes when we reflect on others it causes us to take our mind off of our own pain.

As I write, I am thinking about the olive and how the only way the oil can flow is from the process of being crushed. The oil represents the anointing and power of God which often comes after we have gone through processes which may appear to come into our lives to destroy us, but God says, "Not so... I give and I take away."

Olive Oil can literally lower your risk of heart disease, I correlate this concept to allowing the anointing and oil of God to soothe over a broken heart. It can help take away the pain.

I found out whenever something was taken away, God was able to replace it, fill my emptiness, and give me strength to keep moving ahead even when I felt I could not take another step or breathe.

He let me know I was special to Him, and no one could ever take His place.

Yes, Heavenly Father loved me back to life. I finally realized God did not create my storms, even though I wondered why I had to go through them like when my mother died, or when I was humiliated by failed relationships which He did not ordain for me in the first place. He showed me there was and is an enemy who wants to steal our peace, rob us of our joy, and keep us from reaching our destiny.

It was not God who created these storms full of disappointment and dismay. It was the enemy. An enemy who saw my potential even when I did not. Other times it was my wrong choices. I had to come clean with myself and with God. I mean, who better to trust with disappointments?

I learned the importance of praying for God's will to be done in my life. "Not my will but thine be done." My friend, the enemy's plan is to do everything and anything in his power to cause you and me to take our focus off of God. Yet, we must not allow this to happen. God wants us to concentrate on Him, not on the problem, not on the disappointments, not on our emotions, and not even on our own rationalization.

27"But Jesus spoke to them at once. 'Don't be afraid.' he said. 'Take courage. I am here.' 28Then Peter called to him. "Lord, if it's really you, tell me to come to you, walking on the water." 29Yes, come," Jesus said. So Peter went over the side of the boat and walked on the water toward Jesus. 30But when he saw the strong wind and the waves, he was terrified and began to sink. "Save me, Lord!" he shouted. 31Jesus immediately reached out and grabbed him. "You have so little faith," Jesus said. "Why did you doubt me? (Matthew 14: 27-31)

I, too, felt like Peter, sinking in the sea when I took my focus off of God and placed it on the storm. Yet, I learned crying was not enough, I had to point my petition and affection in an intentional direction and that was towards God.

I had to rely wholeheartedly on God's strength and not my own. I had to watch what I listened to and who I listened to, because it was hard to heal while allowing myself to continuously be wounded.

I had to change my way of thinking and get rid of the thoughts which told me I deserved to be treated how I was being treated and that God was punishing me. I began changing my focus and quoting scriptures of encouragement which spoke about life, love, and the promises of God.

Many times when there was no one to talk to, I found it comforting to journal, which allowed me to get thoughts out of my head and onto paper. These were thoughts which kept me up late at night. I let God know exactly how I felt about everything—no more trying to hide my feelings from a God who sees and knows everything anyway—and after some time, by God's grace, I learned to rely more on God and less on myself.

Yes, we have to be determined and take steps towards better. Through it all, God showed me He was there all of the time. He showed me not everyone was against me and that even in the midst of the "Clear," I was truly not alone.

I have finally accepted some people needed to be cleared out of my life, even if but for a season. It took purposeful reflection and seeking after God's heart to understand and accept this.

After spending time in fervent prayer and fasting, I learned the power of forgiveness and the importance of surrendering my will to God's will. The suffering which Jesus endured on the cross was more than enough to heal my brokenness. The powerful blood which He shed on the cross of Calvary was sufficient for every situation. No more guilt! No more shame!

I discovered in order for me to move forward, it was important for me to learn how to forgive. Forgiving those who offended me freed my mind and emotions from painful memories.

As I started to pray about my trials and offenses, I accepted the fact that human beings can only be human. I started to take my focus off of the persons who caused me pain and learned about the power of forgiveness.

During those difficult moments, the enemy's intent was to cause me to give up on life and to charge our Heavenly Father wrongfully for what he was doing. Yes, I was in the "Clear," in a space where the familiar was unusual and those who I felt should have been there basically cleared out.

Little did I know the "Chief in charge," my Lord and Savior Jesus Christ, was right there all along.

He was watching and waiting for me to invite Him into my suffering, instead of pushing Him away. Although God could have given up on me and abandoned me, He did not. He was faithful, even when I could not sense His presence and when I felt as though my prayers were bouncing off of the ceiling. They were not.

I discovered faith is more than feelings, because feelings change according to circumstances—happy one moment, sad the next, victorious one second and defeated the next. No, instead, God wanted me to trust in His word, which reads, I will never fail you, I will never abandon you. (Hebrews 13:5)

I later discovered, there were people who I did not even know who were praying for me.

There were also those whom I did know who were genuinely concerned, but during that time I came to realize it was not meant for me to depend on them or even on myself for that matter. I needed to depend on God who became more than a faraway distant God whom I read about on the pages of a book.

He became more personal to me than ever before, and like a mother to the motherless, father to the fatherless, and friend to the friendless, He encouraged my soul and filled my longing and broken heart with love.

It was while I was in the "clear," I faced my fears, my failures and my struggles with who I was and who I had become. It was in the "clear," where I found out God deserved all of the glory for any and everything which happened in my life.

He became my Sustainer, my Provider, my Healer, my Helper, my Comforter, and my Strength.

Yes, the "Chief in charge" was in the room bringing me back to life over and over again. He was resuscitating and breathing life back into my dreams, aspirations, and destiny.

I pray you are able to discover the power and comfort of God in the room, if you have not already. I pray you accept the immutable fact that He has not abandoned you, forgotten about you, or "cleared" out. He is not like others. Instead of pulling away when you confront difficulties, He comes very near.

He says, as you and I draw close to Him, He will draw close to us. (James 4:8) God is very present even now regardless of what you may be going through or what sin you may have committed. Tell Him about it; repent; ask for His forgiveness, and spend time with Him. He is there waiting for you to reach out to Him as a child in need of a Father's loving touch.

I also have to mention this: earlier on I was walking down the street and told the Lord if He wanted me to go into the shelter system to see what people experienced, I would. I felt it was part of a bigger calling. I certainly did not go skipping, but nonetheless I had to go.

So if you are reading these words and know you are called to ministry, missions, etc., realize there is a price to be paid. Don't be afraid to gain what you must from the experiences you go through, no matter how they come. Be strong in the power of the Lord and go through. The purpose is much greater than we are. So go through.

May we realize we are not alone, even when it appears we are in the midst of the "clear," the peace, love, and joy that you feel while you are in His presence is like no other experience you have ever known.

He wants you to linger and stay in His presence so that eventually His likeness is seen in you, and you are able to handle life's situations in the way He would...with Victory!

There is still a purpose and reason for us to live, to fulfill our purpose, and to be healed from the hurts of our yesterdays and todays.

The Chief in charge, our Heavenly Father is here and will cause us to triumph in every circumstance as we place our lives in His capable hands. You are victorious now! Onward we go...

CHAPTER 6

I CAN'T SWIM

[15]"...Can a mother forget her nursing child? Can she feel no love for the child she borne? But even if it were possible, I would not forget you.-Isaiah 49:15

I really love this scripture. I guess it brings to mind the many times people go through difficulties and feel utterly alone. I will admit there were times when I felt God had forgotten about me as well. I wondered if I had failed Him or even more, perhaps He did not love me anymore. I now know that was a lie and not the case.

God showed me time and time again, year in and year out He was with me all of the time. I guess this is why the aforementioned scripture touches the core of my being. It is a promise of God I rely on and take to heart on a continual basis.

I would like to share a true story which took place many years ago. I can laugh now, but was not able to laugh at what happened while I was experiencing it.

The scene or might I add fiasco took place during my High School year which involved swimming. For some reason I could not get the hand-foot coordination together.

Nonetheless, I took the class anyway, believing I would finally learn how to swim. In order to pass the class, each student had to swim successfully—yes, successfully—across the entire length of the pool. Well, I was frightened out of my wits! Why you ask?

Well, when I was a child, I had an unforgettable trip to the beach. It was a beautiful sunny day. The seagulls were flying around the blue placid sky, and there were kids playing as their parents sun bathed. As usual, I had sand in my box of popcorn and peanuts, yet all seemed right with the world. I decided to wade in the shallow water and enjoy the warmth of the day. I really liked jumping over the waves as they rolled in swishing, rising, and then subsiding over and over again.

As I enjoyed my playful jumping game, something in the water wrapped around one of my legs. It felt creepy and as if it had a bunch of long, rubber-like legs (probably seaweed). The feeling freaked me out.

I recall taking my mind off the waves to figure out what was in the water, when a surge of water came out of nowhere. The current knocked me off my feet and submerged my body completely under the water.

I couldn't catch my breath! It was such a scary experience. So there I was fighting with the water. You could not tell me that wave had not carried me out to sea. When I finally stood up, I realized I was right at the brink of the sand. The wave had slapped me back toward the edge of the beach. My goodness!

I thought I was drowning, but all I had to do was stand up. Although that happened a long time ago, I had not gotten over the trauma. In my mind, I suffered a tidal wave, a tsunami, yet in reality it was much smaller.

So there I was years later facing my fear and subjecting myself to the torture of swimming. Okay, maybe it was not torture. But I guess my teacher sensed my fear and anxiety. He told me, if I could make it across the length of the pool, he would give me a sixty-five.

"Okay," I thought, "I can't swim on my stomach, but I do know how to swim on my back." I know. Leave it up to me to do the hard part first.

Truthfully, I did not like the feeling of having my head under water. Nevertheless, I did not want to fail the class, so I tried. (I guess you can sense where this is going).

Please know I would love to tell you I passed my swim test with flying colors and started doing the butterfly, doggie paddle, and backstroke as the class cheered; and the teacher started leaping for joy

But no, it was nothing like that at all! There I was on my back heading toward the deep end of the pool, with my hands slightly cupped, guiding the water ever so gently, when for some reason I felt the need to start steering toward the edge of the pool, and then it happened.

I cannot tell you how it happened, but in an instance I discovered I was no longer on my back in a horizontal position. Instead I was in a vertical position. By the time I had a chance to think, down I went.

All I could see was water and bubbles as I sank to the bottom of the pool. Somehow I had made it to the deep end which was about eight feet.

As the water pushed me back up to the surface I could see my fellow students on the other side of the pool looking on watching me and panicking. "Oh my goodness," I thought, "they are looking at me like I am about to drown!" They looked shocked!

I could tell they wanted to help and were waiting for the teacher to give them the okay, but of course, he did no t. Darn teacher.

He was using my catastrophic, embarrassing event as a teaching moment. I guess the only one who learned something that day was the teacher.

Down I went again. More bubbles, more sinking. I wondered, "What possessed the teacher on this day to remain fully clothed in those khaki pants knowing his non-swimming student was going to test that day? I mean, did his optimism give him amnesia and cause him to forget the way the water bullied me? We actually had a fight almost every day. Yes, that water was like, "Oh you're back again?"

So there was Mr. Khaki pants, on the side of the pool, fully clothed and waiting for me to pull it together, and all I could think was, "I CAN'T SWIM!"

"HELP!" I thought. "This is not the time to try to use this experience to see if I will get it. Just come and get me out of this water! This is not Psychology. This is my life!"

All I can say is both the teacher and his khaki pants almost ended up in the pool that day, because when he reached out to help me, I practically climbed up his arm like a cat trying to escape from a tub of water. Unbeknownst to my swim teacher, he became a firetruck that day and his arm became my rescue ladder.

I can still see him in my mind telling me, "Relax, Relax!" I wanted to say, "Man please. Relax? I almost died today trying to get a sixty-five! You relax, Mr. Khaki pants and give me my sixty-five while you're at it!"

The good news was, at least he gave me a sixty-five for almost drowning and making a spectacle of myself. So as much as I would love to tell you I learned how to swim that day and went on to start a school where I now teach young children to overcome their fear of swimming—I can't.

I can chuckle about this story today. But back then, it certainly was no laughing matter.

Life can sometimes seem like that pool experience, where our struggles resemble the current which engulfed me as a child. Sometimes, we find ourselves trying to catch our breath with arms flailing and bubbles churning as we fight to come up for air.

But then here comes another challenge, and back down again we go.

I am not sure of what your "current" is. It could be a "current" situation which has you or someone you love panicking. It could be a broken relationship, grief, abuse, illness or even financial pressure. Yet, I want to remind you of the words in the scripture above wherein God states, "I will not forget you!"

Your struggle may be great, you may feel depleted of strength, even as if the pressure is trying to pull you under.

But those feelings will dissipate as you put your hope and trust in our Heavenly Father who does not leave us even when we feel alone.

When you go through deep waters, I will be with you. When you go through rivers of difficulty you will not drown. When you walk through the fire of oppression, you will not be burned up; the flames will not consume you. (Isaiah 43:2)

Although for some, this scripture may not be literal, we can take comfort in knowing that whatever state we find ourselves in, God will not allow it to overtake us. I thought my life was over that day, but even when I did not know to pray, God was still there protecting me. I felt the water trying to consume me, but God would not allow it.

I urge you to keep on working at it. Have faith and keep on resting in God's promises. Keep on knowing you do not have to give up on your hopes, dreams, and aspirations. The problems of life will not consume you.

"Don't give up!" God does have a purpose for your life and He has not forgotten about you!

CHAPTER 7

SWEETNESS AND GRANDMA WISDOM

This story is written in memory of my late praying grandmother and grandparents everywhere. Grandma was not much like the character depicted in this story, yet she was constant in prayer. Her prayer life prompted a conversation with me which I truly believe saved my life. Please know the subject matter in this story is no laughing matter, however, I took an opportunity to incorporate a little humor, a little truth, and a lot of hope to lighten the content. Enjoy!

²Worship the Lord with gladness. Come before him, singing with joy. ³Acknowledge that the Lord is God! He made us, and we are his. (Psalm 100:2-3)

I would like to share a true story of two beautiful young ladies who did not know how precious their lives were to God. I will refer to them as Sweetness and Rose Petal—and so the story begins.

Sweetness and Rose Petal were the very best of friends. The girls did almost everything together, were very much like sisters, and spent a great deal of time sharing, laughing, and talking about their young, but complicated lives.

One day during their many private talks, Rose Petal told Sweetness a secret. One which caused her great embarrassment and humiliation. A secret she was too embarrassed to share with anyone else.

Rose Petal told Sweetness her dad was touching her in ways which made her feel uncomfortable and unloved. She shared feelings of confusion and how she did not understand why or how he could do this to her.

Sweetness was very sad for her friend. She identified with Rose Petal's feelings of shame and fear. She too had experienced the same devastation associated with perversion and molestation.

Because of Rose Petal's honesty, Sweetness also shared an emotional story. She told of how she too had been fondled in the middle of the night and made to touch her relative in ways which made her feel ashamed, disgusted, and confused. Confused, because she could not understand why something that was so wrong aroused her. Yet, she additionally felt scared, filthy, and disgusted to the point she wanted to vomit.

She did not understand the body was created with certain arousal points that were specifically for an appointed time in marriage, and had nothing to do with someone taking advantage of her innocence. There was a special time, when those feelings could be shared and enjoyed with her spouse.

Sweetness stated she felt scared, because her relative told her he would deny the story if she ever shared it, and even went as far as to threaten her. She expressed how she shuddered each time he would say, "This is our little secret."

Many times he would make her feel as though the molestation was her fault, although the abuse started when she was very young. The truth was he knew Sweetness loved her mother and never wanted to do anything to hurt or make her angry. How she hated keeping the abuse from her mother. Yet, his constant intimidations left her feeling as though she had no other choice than to remain silent.

Both girls wondered if the abuse was their fault and if they had done something to cause the mistreatment. Poor Sweetness. Poor Rose Petal.

As the girls sat and talked they realized they had a great deal in common and thought it best to take matters into their own hands.

They knew their mothers and family loved them, but at that time, their sadness overshadowed their happy moments with family and friends. Regretfully they made an appointment to take their lives.

Although afraid, they felt good about their decision, as they did not know how to make the abuse stop and sadly believed suicide was the best option. At least they could spend time together and still be best friends on the other side, they thought. Little did they know someone else was watching them and had another plan.

For I know the plans I have for you," says the Lord. They are plans for good and not for disaster, to give you a future and a hope. 12In those days when you pray, I will listen.13If you look for me wholeheartedly, you will find me.14I will be found by you," says the Lord. "I will end your captivity and restore your fortunes. (Jeremiah 29:11, NLV)

Saturday rolled around and Sweetness was ready to meet with Rose Petal when her mother entered the room. "Hi baby," she said. "Get your things ready, we are going to see your grand-mommy."

"What?" thought Sweetness. "No Way!"

She was surprised and disappointed all at the same time. "See!" she thought, placing her hand over her mouth to silence the thoughts screaming oh so loudly inside of her head.

"Did you say something, Hun?" asked her mother.

"Uhhh, no mommy," answered Sweetness. But deep inside she couldn't help but think, "Grandma Wisdom is at it again!"

Don't get me wrong; Sweetness loved her grandmother, but she also loved Rose Petal and did not want to let her down. However, she knew better than to tell her mother "No."

Truthfully, there was a little something about Grandma Wisdom that downright frightened Sweetness and made her feel really uncomfortable.

For one, Grandma Wisdom kept her teeth in a glass on her nightstand. To Sweetness, they seemed a little eerie, because they looked like they were constantly smiling at her every time she walked past the bedroom. She would oftentimes try to dart past her grandmother's room in order to not get a glimpse of those teeth. I mean the dentures did not have eyes, yet she always felt like they were following her.

Then there were those thick, black bifocals which made Grandma Wisdom's beady eyes seem larger than life, and Sweetness shuddered as she thought of the black eyed peas which were probably already cooking on the stove. Yuck!!! You know, the ones which were seasoned with hog mars... hog mas...hog moss...well you know what I mean. For the life of her, Sweetness just could not understand why anyone would want to put that stuff in their food.

So on to Grandmother's house, she reluctantly went. Grandma Wisdom was a short, stout woman whose electric white hair, sat at attention piled on the top of her head. She looked as if she had been struck by lightning—white lightning from Heaven.

Grandma Wisdom's eyes resembled two shiny dark marbles, which made Sweetness feel as if she were trying to pierce into the depths of her soul to see if she was lying about...well, anything. She had a way of making Sweetness feel guilty like she had committed some crime or something even when she had not.

"Sweetness," Grandma Wisdom would say, "God don't like liars, so don't even thinks 'bout lying to me." Sweetness would often jokingly tell her friends Grandma Wisdom had the "Hook-up to Heaven," and although she was posing as a grandmother, she was actually an undercover Senior Citizen superhero with x-ray vision and supersonic ears which allowed her to hear over bridges, tunnels, state lines, oceans and everything in between.

Sweetness was even afraid of cutting class. She just knew her supersonic hero of a grandma would find out, and the rest would make the history books or maybe a comic book.

Can you picture Grandma Wisdom with those stout little legs, in her plaid housedress, braids plaited in the air going boing...boing...boing? You could just imagine her in that strong Southern dialect which quickly turned Bajan when she was upset saying, "Sweetnesscomovae'r anlemmegitchagial!" (Translation: Sweetness come over here and let me get you girl!)

"I don't know how she knows," Sweetness would say with her hands in the air and her eyes stretched wide in disbelief, "but she knows almost everything, even if I don't tell her! Man – I can't get away with nothing!"

By the time Sweetness and her mother arrived at her grandmother's, she realized she had not called Rose Petal. "Oh no," she thought.

As Grandma Wisdom opened the door, the smell of fresh, warm buttered biscuits soothingly invited Sweetness in like a warm cup of chamomile tea with honey.

"Thank goodness," thought Sweetness, "no beans." Despite her complaining, she really enjoyed feeling the comforting embrace of Grandma Wisdom's arms, which made her feel as if she were being hugged by a mama bear, wrapped in a warm housecoat drenched in fabric softener.

"Come on here baby," said Grandma Wisdom after plopping a dry kiss on Sweetness' face. "Settle in and meet me in the kitchen."

"Oh, here we go," thought Sweetness, "she is going to start making me read from her 'good book.'" She quickly scooted past Grandma Wisdom's bedroom to avoid "The Teeth."

As she sat down she could sense something was up. Then it happened. You know "it," that thing I told you about. Grandma Wisdom was at "it" again and when she spoke, the words practically caused Sweetness to fall from her chair.

"You know Sweetness...," said Grandma Wisdom without even turning to face Sweetness as she wiped her brow on the back of her hand while holding the dishwashing towel, "If you commit suicide, God will not forgive you, and you will go straight to hell."

"What?" yelled Sweetness? *Aww man the hook up is happening! Heaven must have called her before I got here.* "I mean, yes, ma'am," said Sweetness sheepishly. See this is exactly what I was talking about. She's doing it again.

The last thing Sweetness wanted to do was go to hell. She was actually frightened of it—fire, brimstone, screaming and gnashing of teeth, eternal suffering. No way, thought Sweetness. I don't know if hell is real or not, but I'm certainly not taking any chances.

That was the day, Sweetness realized there was another plan, a bigger and better plan for her life. God used her praying hooked up-to-Heaven, biscuit making, and Super-Senior hero of a grandmother to stop a plan which was not to be. Now that's powerful! Go on grandma!

Later on Sweetness came to know the God of her grandmother who loved her so much. A grandmother who prayed at all times of the day and night. She truly believed God would hear her petition and save her family.

Sweetness, of course, told Rose Petal about what happened, and both girls vowed to never discuss taking their lives again and even told their moms about what they had experienced and what they planned to do. But that was no more.

Things changed for the better for the girls and they discovered they had nothing to fear as they placed their faith and hope in the God of Grandma Wisdom. They discovered God had a plan for their lives and that His love, grace, and mercy were available to help and heal them.

My friend, I do not know if you have ever contemplated suicide, or if the enemy of your soul has caused you to feel as if there is or was no reason for you to live. Well, I want you to know this is not true. You have every right to live as the next person. Even if you suffered molestation, I want you to know it was not your fault.

The words of your loving Father are penned in one of the greatest books known to man. This Book speaks of His great love for you and how He is able to cause you to triumph despite the hopeless and unappreciated moments you have faced and may currently be facing. This book is called the Holy Bible and although there are different interpretations the message of God's' love and power, supersede any superficial reasons for not searching the pages. It's a spiritual thing.

God is not shocked by anything we face and His word does not change according to our circumstance; it remains the same even in the most difficult of trials.

Sweetness discovered her Heavenly Father promised her life and His Spirit would comfort her in every situation. God had a purpose for the girls despite the enemies plan to derail them.

The more her grandmother prayed for her, the more the enemy tried to thwart those prayers and prevent her from discovering God's love for her. But God intervened on her behalf anyway.

Sweetness learned she never had to keep uncomfortable secrets from her mother and that God would give her the strength to overcome any challenge she faced in life. She was not alone. She no longer had to cry silent tears.

Some of the tactics the enemy uses against us are discouragement, low-self-esteem, bullying, lies and rejection. These are some of the strongest weapons he uses against you and me.

Yet, God sends His word of comfort that says, "But in that coming day no weapon turned against you will succeed. You will silence every voice raised up to accuse you. These benefits are enjoyed by the servants of the Lord; their vindication will come from me. I, the Lord, have spoken!" (Isaiah 54:17).

Yes, as we place our trust in the promises of God, He will give us strength to overcome. He has a purpose and plan for our lives, and we must press forward and trust God to experience them.

If you have lost someone to suicide, my prayers are with you. Please know Grandma Wisdom's response is what helped me in my early teens. Although Grandma Wisdom is a fictitious character, the fact still remains my grandmother prayed and used her "hook-up to Heaven" to let me know God had another plan for my life.

I want to say this as well, only God knows what a person says in their final moments and if you have lost someone to suicide, I pray your loved one found a way in to His presence. I pray you find solace in knowing God sees our tears and heals the brokenness of those who mourn.

If you are reading this book and are the molester I pray you run and get help as fast as you can. Even through the guilt, shame and embarrassment, find someone to help. Someone will listen. Truth is many Molesters have been molested themselves, but may not have had the chance to share their experience of violation. Just because you never told anyone does not mean the feelings of fear and hurt are gone.

God is a healer, but when we offend and do things contrary to God's will for our lives, we must repent, which means turning away from the wrong. If you believe, He will show you how. Seek help as soon as you can as there is something terribly wrong with violating a child. Children are innocent and they trust you. Please don't take their trust for granted.

May we continue moving forward knowing we were created for God's plan and purpose.

Though sometimes broken and discouraged may we continue releasing our burdens to Him. He is the Mender of the wounded heart and broken spirit. Here's to releasing the pain and moving forward.

Let's move on...

CHAPTER 8

DOES FOSTER CARE?

" Really? Tell me more," he said. "Honestly babe, it's a little hard for me talk about, but okay..." she said shyly. "I remember Caroline she used to make the best brownies, so moist and chocolatey.

Oh, and then there was Dillard. He was a mess! I think he wanted to drive us a little insane. He would literally grab our heads, place them underneath his backside, and then fart on us. I hated that, but I felt there was nothing any of us little ones could do to make him stop. We were Dillard's little play toys. He was so much bigger than us and used his weight to prove it, our foster big brother, "Large and in charge."

She stared off in the distance as if looking at a picture on the wall while recollecting memories too painful to remember, yet too intense to forget.

There were a few other little ones there too. I cannot remember their names anymore, but what I do recall is when I first met the Fosters, they seemed like such a nice married couple. I guess this is why I could not understand why they did things to hurt and frighten us.

For instance, there were days we were forced to watch horror movies on a super large screen in the basement. I can still remember the sounds, screams and pictures. It was just too much for a four-year-old to have to deal with.

I really don't understand what type of satisfaction they received from embedding fear inside of us. There were days we were 'whipped' with extension cords.

They would tell us to line up in the basement for our beatings from the smallest to the tallest. It didn't matter the size, the age, or if you did not do anything wrong—everyone got a whack. It stung worse than anything I could imagine, and felt like my skin was being ripped from my body. I tried not to scream in agony, but the pain would overtake me until I shuddered in anguish.

I wondered why they were torturing me when I was such a quiet and well-behaved child.

I remember the day Mr. Foster or "Foster," as the older children called him, was out front with his shovel, a shovel which seemed so enormous next to my small and thin frame. I can recall the sky was very dark that night and seemed as if it literally was engulfing me. I felt I could touch it if I stood on my tippy toes.

Mr. Foster called all of the children over as he continued to dig. By now the hole was large enough for a few of us to fit into and appeared as a never-ending abyss of gloom.

I wondered, why was he digging such a large hole in the first place and what was it for?

One thing I did know was it made me feel very uncomfortable. When we asked Foster why he was digging it, he told us, he was digging the hole because he wanted to reach the enemy. I was terrified.

Thankfully, shortly after that day I remembered being taken to my mom for a visit. We usually met in a space which had beautifully painted yellow, green, and pink sunflowers on the walls. Oh yes, and they had plenty of toys.

I was so happy to see my mom. I wondered why I was not able to stay with her and why I had to go back to the Fosters who abused us until our skin was raw. It was then I did the only thing I knew to do. "Mommy, please don't make me go back, they beat us so bad. Please, don't make me go back." It was then mommy looked at my back and her face displayed nothing but anger and extreme remorse.

To tell you the truth I don't remember very much of what happened after, but I do remember living with mom after that.

I now know it was not that mommy did not love me or my brother, but that she was young and at the time thought it would be best to place my brother and I with a family who she felt was better equipped financially to raise us. I totally get it now.

I always wondered what ever happened to the other children who were left to stay with the Fosters. I wonder if they felt like me as a child when I questioned, "Does Foster care?"

Did Foster care about us or the money? Why couldn't the Fosters realize they were breaking us in ways which we could not express as children, but would one day struggle with as adults?

I wondered if the other children even made it out of there alive and if that gaping hole Mr. Foster was digging was being created for some other reason. During that time I remembered one of the girls telling me she would pray to her Heavenly Father whenever she felt afraid. I did not really know how to pray at the time, nor did I know who Heavenly Father was. Yet, she kept telling me there were happy times in the world and sad times, but wherever we found ourselves, Heavenly Father would give us the strength we needed to live through it all. She told me. Heavenly Father comforted her and let her know He was with her through it all and there would be better days ahead.

Now that I am older I realize the importance of talking to my Heavenly Father not just when there is trouble, but also when things are going well. I have met other children who were in foster homes and have a better understanding of the benefit of foster homes.

I have found out there are wonderful families who take children in and love them as their own.

There are also those who make choices to harm and not help, but regardless, we never have to allow the pain or offence of others to dictate our future and cause us to feel as if there is no hope. We have a Heavenly Father who will never abandon or forsake us.

When we feel threatened we have every right to boldly and openly cry out and ask for help until someone listens. As I learned to pray and give my hurt, insecurities, fears, and failures to Heavenly Father, I discovered He was able to heal my brokenness and sustain me through heartache and grief.

I am so glad I found the strength to speak up and tell my mom what was going on that day. I believe my mother discovered she was actually able to be a great mom. She did the best she could, she just needed to believe in herself and trust in God.

I also realize being a parent is easier said than done as some parents do not have support, know how to ask for help (sometimes due to disappointment), or know which resources are available to them. Either way we have to keep pressing.

Perhaps you are a child who has lived in a foster home and had a negative experience. Perhaps you were beaten harshly, made to feel you were unloved, and treated unjustly and unfairly; I pray you are no longer in that situation and if you are, I pray you find the courage to talk about it. I pray someone will listen to you and help you, even if you have to keep asking until you find the right person.

Realize you were made to be loved and cherished. May you find comfort in knowing you are loved this day and your Heavenly Father sees you and loves you right where you are today. I pray the voices of your naysayers become obsolete and the sting of the past be nothing more than a testimony. I pray God's voice be bigger than the naysayers and all those who don't appreciate you for who you are.

I pray you never allow the pain of your past to dictate the hope of your future.

I pray you are able to hear the wonderful things the Lord says about you. I pray God's voice will be the biggest, brightest, and strongest voice in your heart. A voice which celebrates and adores you.

Keep looking, keep searching, keep hoping, keep praying, and please don't give up!

CHAPTER 9

GOD DOESN'T THROW AWAY BROKEN THINGS

Yes, my scars you can see
Yet, instead of giving empathy you call me, "Crazy"
You see my tears and minimize my insecurities and fears
Tell truth and lies, hellos and goodbyes

Embraces, releases,
Let go from friendly foes
Sweet nothings and I don't knows
Gains and losses, of employees and bosses

Yet I, although once shattered
Physically broken, mentally scattered

The pain, well pretty much the same
Loss, identity, and name
Yet you say I am to blame for my error and choices

You say I lack smarts and savviness, so you consider me less
Say my smiles are a consequence of my being unlevelled, elevator
broken

Yet, my smile is how I overcome intense pain
My way of finding solace in the rain
Of walking, still, amidst the pain
Of standing while crippled, of placid waters now rippled

Of a life now changed, just from learning a name
One encounter, turned to years
Of I told you so, instead of cheers
Yet, it's true when I reminisce on how long I conquered even this
I realize I am a reflection of grace

Please don't take the liberty of calling me out of my name
I was not born to reflect your fame
Neither am I a stepping stool for the cruel and those who rule

But I was created for Him and by Him
And because of Him I am still here
Through hurt and despair
In spite of every care
All I can say is He won't throw me away
I am Alive to strive, to thrive and survive
I am still here, once broken, but comforted in knowing
He won't throw me away

There are days when you may feel like giving up, times when you will ask yourself again and again, "How long?" "How long will I have to put up with being treated unfairly, being misunderstood and underappreciated?"

There will be moments when you will wonder, "Why do I keep coming in contact with people who do not have my best interest at heart?"

You may even wonder if God still cares. He does.

There will be instances when you will not only want to throw in the towel, but the washcloth, the soap, and everything else. Your challenges will cause you to question your purpose and wonder, "Will things ever get better?"

Ever ask yourself, "How did I get here?"

If you can allow yourself the freedom to focus on God's Word along with the wonderful, positive, and loving things He says about you, you will learn to abort and deny the lies the enemy has placed in your mind.

Please know that God uses broken people who have gone through some of the most traumatic events in life. Your destiny is not predicated on how you feel about yourself or even by the ill feelings others have towards you.

I can recall being in a place where while the worship was happening, in the midst of the praises, I could hear the sound of brokenness. It sounded like fine China crumbling to the ground.

I know the thoughts I think towards you, saith the Lord; thoughts of peace and not of evil to give you a hope and a future. (Jeremiah 29:11)

What are your thoughts saying about you right now? Our advancement, growth and outlook on life is oftentimes based on loving and focusing on God.

When it comes to encouragement and victorious living, sometimes you will have to search for it, other times reach for it, but most of all you will have to trust in the God of creation to bring you to it.

You will have to believe in the God who tells the storms to cease. The God who is greater than opposition and feelings of defeat. He is superior to our failures.

He is stronger than our foes and enemies.

More magnificent than our financial struggles. Greater than the boss who may not see your potential. Greater than the employee who may not give their all. Greater than the person who hurt you or ridiculed you. Greater than those who used you and then called you crazy.

God is greater than your past. Greater than your present and future. He is all encompassing, all knowing, and all forgiving. He is wiser than the wisest. He is greater than the greatest. But even in all of His glory, splendor, majesty, and might, He, unlike others, does not throw away broken things.

I love this about God. He sees our brokenness and imperfections, but does not get rid of us.

No, instead He uses broken people, people who have gone through some of the most traumatic events in life, to rise, to shine, and to be a blessing to others.

Someway, somehow, He puts us back together again. Occasionally, the mending is solely physical, but often it is emotional and even mental.

He heals the brokenhearted and bandages their wounds. (Psalm 147:3)

Ever read a really good book? At first the pages are nice and crisp, but after they go through being turned and manipulated in various ways, they start to appear frayed, wrinkled, and even discolored.

Perhaps the book may have been left in the sun and the pages appear tarnished.

Maybe the book is handled by someone who does not know how to handle a good book and the book becomes torn.

Regardless of the how the package has changed, the message is still clear—it's a good book, a good story, waiting to be discovered and appreciated.

What is your story my friend? Have you ever been broken? If so, I will admit, it can be difficult sharing our heart and failures with others, yet companionship, relationship, community and support along with the strength of God, are essential in moving forward towards hope and healing.

God will not abandon you. On the contraire, He will be with you during the process.

He will not reject you, but will love you as you continue to place your trust in Him. If someone has abandoned you, please don't lose hope. Cry when you need to as your pain is real, but it also helps to pour your concern and disappointment in God's direction. Take time to breathe and be kind to yourself. Find ways to rest in God's presence and if you are able, find people who have your best interest at heart; perhaps, a prayer partner or someone who loves God and knows how to encourage you. Sometimes I even treat myself to a scoop of ice-cream or buy my favorite fruit.

Other times I may sit in the park by the lake and watch the ducks or spend quality time with family. Be intentional about making time to soak in God's presence while meditating on His word. This practice can give a much needed break from the stressors and noise of everyday life.

Personally, there were times when I had to re-evaluate my surroundings. There were moments when I needed to hide in God's secret place in order to be restored. I cleaned out my social media platform and became more mindful of personal acquaintances.

I became more aware of God's great love for me. I am constantly learning about the compassion of our Heavenly Father. He really does want the best for His children.

Your heart will heal as you place your hope and trust in God.

5Trust in the LORD with all your heart; do not depend on your own understanding. 6Seek his will in all you do, and he will show you which path to take. - (Proverbs 3:5-6)

Your brokenness is only temporary. You have to know and believe God is in control and has better for your life. Reach out by faith. Take time to see yourself in a better place. God is able to not only put us back together again, but to restore us and to command the storms to cease as found in Matthew 8:23-27. I am declaring and believing for brighter days ahead."

Never settle, always remember the Father's love is great for you, and He does not throw away broken things. He will meet you where you are, but will never leave you there. Take heart and be strong.

Let's go on from here...

CHAPTER 10

GOD WHO WALKS IN THE GARDEN

When I was a little girl, I loved to touch and smell beautiful flowers. I immensely enjoyed the boastful scent of the lily, brightness of the sunflower, and splendor of the rose which seemed to illuminate the entire atmosphere with glory and splendor.

I enjoyed taking strolls in the garden while birds chirped and flew playfully in and out of flowers, while sipping on remnants of rain left from a passing shower. Ahh, the garden!

Some days I would walk while breathing in deeply and allowing the aroma of the flowers to completely engulf me, while filling my lungs with fresh, calming aromas. Mmm, lavender, my favorite.

Have you ever walked through a garden and experienced its glory and tranquility?

I have, and while there, I imagined each flower as a child decked out in their colorful outfit for the first day of school... bending and twisting, while beckoning, "Look at me! Look at me!"

I can recall a warm breeze blowing ever so gently on the petals as the flowers appeared to dance playfully in the wind as butterflies fluttered happily through yellow dandelions, pink begonias, and purple lavender.

The sight, the sound, and the smell—such bliss. Yet, just as there were serene, sun-filled moments, there were also instances when darkened clouds hid the inviting, rays of the sun. Days when thunder bellowed far off in the distance.

To this end, the flowers which once appeared to dance and sway, now bowed their seeming-like heads in humble submission, while closing their petals in preparation for the inevitable – the storm.

Truthfully, there are moments when we, too, like the flowers of the garden stand strong and sway calmly in the breeze of life without much care. But there are also days when storms arise and we bow and brace for the impending storm.

Storms which threaten our peace and attempt to place our emotions in a cataclysmic abyss of chaos. During these storms, the once light pitter-pattering raindrops, become a torrential downpour which causes us to cringe and wonder with uncertainty. How long? Storms of divorce, financial strains, foreclosures, evictions, loss of loved ones, and the like, cause us to weep while hoping we do not snap under the weight of such intense pressure.

We continue to look up and wonder how long the sun will be hidden behind the clouds. When will we see and feel its warmth? Soon we hope.

Then finally, a glimmer of hope as the clouds start to move off in the distance and there it is, shining ever so brightly—the sun!

Truthfully, the sun never moved, the storm simply obstructed its view. Which leads me to the following questions;

Does the Almighty God, our Heavenly Father, who loves us more than we know, leave us when we go through difficulties?

Does He turn a deaf ear to our cries during our darkest moments? Does He shut His eyes and become blinded to our pain? The answer is, "No!" I say this with emphasis because I am reminded of the countless people who have been lied to and led to believe God has forgotten about them.

These are people who have experienced great sickness, pressure and the like. Some have become so devastated they resorted to ending their lives.

Their deaths not only make me sad, but angry because I know all too well about the lies of the enemy, which tells us God caused the pain, which is not true.

It is the enemy who whispers in our ears and tells us God no longer loves us or wants us because of failures or sins we have committed. He tells us God hates us and has turned His back on us.

I too have experienced days and even months when I wondered if God had forgotten about me.

I now know any time we allow anyone or anything to become our primary source of happiness while pushing God to the back, that person or thing becomes our idol. Doing so many times points us in the direction for difficult times. Yet, when I had enough and decided to place God first and humbled myself before Him, things changed. I had to make a decision, to give the Lord my heart, soul, mind and everything else.

For me, there was no more hiding and giving God a part of me (the part of me I thought was worthy). I poured out my tears, my emotions and complaint before him and found out the suffering of Jesus Christ on the cross was and is greater than our sin and failure, greater than the enemy's lies and attacks, greater than anything we can ever imagine.

God does not abandon us in times of crises. He is there to help us and to give us the strength we need to go through the difficulties of life. The God of the garden is also the Lily of the Valley. He is not just with us when the sun is shining and all things appear to be going well. No, He is not a God who loves only those who look good, smell good, and have money in their pocket.

His love is not selfish; it is immeasurable. He does not respect or prefer one group of people or one person over another. His love is above all and available to all.

Even when others have forsaken you, He is faithful still. Even if you have forsaken God, His love is available, and He reaches to us by His Spirit and tells us it is all right to share our pain, anguish, and disappointment with Him.

He wants us to come to Him in whatever state we find ourselves and to love Him with our whole heart. His love is not predicated on how others feel about us. He does not love us when others love us and then leave us when others turn away. His love is constant and true.

He is even with us in the rain; for when it comes, the showers often water the roots and give strength to the stem and plant at large, causing it to stand strong and flourish in its season. I don't know how it happens, but somehow, by the grace of God we stand taller as we allow the Son to walk with us in the rain.

Although I am not particularly referring to rains of utter destruction, I am here to say God has ways of using some of the things which the enemy meant for our destruction as a catalyst to open our understanding and to raise us up to the next level.

It was in my most uncomfortable moments that I discovered the greatness, the mercy, and the compassion of God. The gratitude I thought I had for God prior to the storm did not amount to what I feel now, knowing He has been constant and true.

He has supplied my needs and taken me from here to there and there to here. Through depths of sadness and depression to heights of joy where I laugh at adversity, I have realized happiness is often predicated by what is happening in our lives at that moment and is not constant. Joy comes straight from the fountain of Heaven, *and the joy of the Lord is my strength* (Nehemiah 8:10)

Therefore, I pray you find ways to dance in the rain like the lilies in the garden while knowing God is with you and you are never alone.

He is your constant and true friend. Lean on Him, hope in Him and keep looking ahead.

Forward we go...

CHAPTER 11

A DIFFERENT KIND OF PASSION

Lately, I have been hearing a great deal of talk regarding the fulfillment of dreams, purposes, and passion. Yet, I have discovered many are not sure of what their passion actually is.

(What? No passion?) Before knowing what we are passionate about, it helps to define the word passion. According to the Merriam Webster dictionary. passion is "a strong feeling or enthusiasm or excitement for something or about doing something."

Truthfully, each and every one of us displays some form of passion on a daily basis without even knowing it. For instance, we are passionate about getting up in the morning, even when we do not want to, and passionate about making breakfast and dinner taste yummy.

Some are passionate about their living space and belonging's, others about family. Many parents are passionate about raising children even if it means placing personal dreams on hold. We are oftentimes passionate about life and finding ways to make things better, even if circumstances seem to be getting worse.

Passion is the reason we keep looking for changes, even when opportunities appear to be closed in our face.

Passion and persistence will cause you to look your child in the eye and tell them not to worry, even when you don't know how things will turn out.

Passion is finding ways to make things happen when bills are due and you don't know where the money is going to come from.

Passion and resilience will cause you to keep forging ahead, because you know a change has to come. Passion is looking with expectancy for things to get better each and every day of your life when you do not see how they will.

Passion is learning how to sing and dance while standing in the rain.

Passion is learning to use your voice while speaking up for what you know is right. Passion is standing up for those who cannot stand up for themselves.

Passion is believing things will only get better if you fight for what you believe in and that often means believing in God first and then believing in yourself. Passion is upholding and respecting the unit of family, even if those around you do not think family is important. Stand up for it anyway!

Passion will cause you to reject thoughts of defeat and dust off ashes of brokenness while allowing the promises of God to heal you and give you courage for every situation in life.

So the next time you wonder if you have a passion for anything, do not look for an outside or external voice to validate you. Rather, allow Holy Spirit to instruct you while the inner warrior rises up within you and gives you grace and power to do your God-given positive tasks, even as minuscule as they may seem.

The more you realize and accept the truth of your passion, the more you will find a reason to celebrate your today and the blessing which is found in your everyday living.

So go ahead, you passionate soldier who has not given up and will not give up! I am rooting for you and celebrating with you for where you are right now, where you have been and where you are going.

Allow God to cultivate your life and even the gifts and talents He has entrusted to you. You were made to soar like the eagle who braces for the storm and rises above the turbulence.

There is more to you and your story than many know. You are invaluable! Go ahead, get some pom-poms and celebrate!

Here's to forging ahead!

CHAPTER 12

HELP ME I'VE FALLEN

Can you believe this? The book is finally finished! Yippee! Well not quite finished...

I was super excited. Don't get me wrong, I love writing, but I started feeling as though I was writing "The Never, Ever, Ending, Endingness of Neverendingness..." book. So, by now I was backflip, pirouette, two finger snaps with a head tilt ready to be finished.

Finally, the last chapter...

By now friends were giving me salutations of "Finish that book" instead of saying "Goodbye." Even my daughter joined the bandwagon. I can still hear her in that cute high pitched voice saying, "Mommy, God wants you to finish this book."

"You too?" I thought while chuckling to myself, *Mommy is almost finished. Almost.*

So there I was right at the finish line, close enough to smell freshly printed pages when a screech moment happened as a thought popped into my mind, *you have to write more, you need to add one more chapter.* (Wait whuh?)

Gosh, I thought ... *Really??* Of course, I pulled out the computer and started typing. I have learned the importance of paying attention to the still small voice of God. The expression which tugs at your heart, while telling you to DO something or NOT TO DO something.

So here it is: This story is for those who have fallen - literally, physically/or figuratively. It's time to rise up!

We all fall at one time or another and because the fall can seem so traumatic we often become hesitant about getting up and trying again.

I have come to know one of the most important lessons we learn in life is not focusing on the fall (although it may hurt and cause some embarrassment) but on getting up from the fall.

Simply put, falling is not easy and getting up can be even harder—but worth it!

If you have ever learned to ride a bike or been on roller skates, you may understand what I mean when I say, "Falling is not easy." My first pair of skates were the metal ones which slipped over your sneakers and attached with leather bands and a buckle (I know I am dating myself).

Back then I would scoot around with one skate on just to make sure I did not fall. But that was not skating; that was scooting.

In order for me to really learn how to skate I had to take a chance, put both skates on, and risk falling not once, not twice, but perhaps a few times. Or, at least until I became better at skating.

I will admit I was a very good skater, I even taught myself to jump double-dutch with roller skates on. But in the beginning, scuffed up knees and elbows usually accompanied falls.

However, falling was as integral part of the learning process. Ultimately, I just needed someone to share their expertise. Stand, fall, repeat. This reminds me of an experience I had with falling which I will never forget.

I think I was about fifteen years old—a mama's girl who was relatively shy, petite, and super polite. I spent a great deal of time studying, writing, and singing. I sang so much until I started talk-singing. A few friends told me I still do this (you know who you are). Of course I am smiling.

During my childhood I hated getting in trouble because my mother did not play. She was about four feet and eleven inches tall, yet her strong and assertive personality made her appear to be at least six feet. For this reason, I knew better than to be disobedient, sassy, or disrespectful. Needless to say, I worked really hard at not getting caught. *Save that sass for your friends.*

What I loved about my mother was she was super humorous. Some of the things she would come up with made me laugh until my jaw and stomach hurt. She was also protective and stern. Let us just say, Mommy knew how to switch it up.

I was the youngest of two and remembered thinking Mommy seemed a bit controlling, but now that I am older and have a child of my own, I totally get it. I have come to know parenting is one of the most beautiful, challenging, and loving responsibilities a person could ever have.

So I saw my mother working really hard to make things happen for my brother and me. My dad, Shelton Jackson, passed when I was very young, so I saw my mother as a strong single parent who made sure we were well taken care of.

So I worked really hard at trying to please her.

Moreover, I didn't like getting in trouble, but when I did I would get "the look." You know "the look" which spoke louder than words while screaming at you silently and letting you know "You better pull it together real fast."

When my mother's head turned in my direction and that right eye opened wide enough for me to see her thoughts, I knew it was time to straighten up, sit up, shut up, and get it together... UP! Okay, okay, but I was on a roll.

Because I was so shy and a Creative, I could have done without going outside. I loved being indoors and listening to music. Of course, I played outdoors with my friends, but I was a mommy's girl, so I was content with staying home. I could literally write and sing for hours.

My mother knew how much I loved music, so I was more than excited when I received a small record player with albums to accompany (I know dating myself again). I enjoyed various genres of music including: classical pop, rock and rhythm and blues.

I would play my albums over and over again, while writing the lyrics, and imitating each artist until I felt I had the song down pat. I just loved music! This was my normal routine day in and day out. Music, music, and did I say...music?

However, there were days when my mother would put a halt to my daily routine and strongly encourage, or should I say, command me to go outside.

"Yedidah! Why don't you go outside and get some air!" she would say.

I always wondered, "Why did I have to go outside to get air, when there was air inside?" But I guess all of that singing was wearing my mother out. (Moms need "time outs," or should I say, "quiet time," too). So I got the message and went outside to get some "air."

Normally, I would stay in the neighborhood, but on this particular day, my best friend asked me to go with her to visit her... boyfriend. Ooh boyfriend!!! Of course I was such a good friend I could not refuse.

She was my best friend, and we did almost everything together, plus her boyfriend had a brother.

Before I knew it we were on the train heading to a faraway land. At least it seemed that way.

As a matter of fact, the ride was so long I felt we were going to Georgia. Did I mention I did not tell my mother I was leaving the neighborhood?

But then again, why did I have to tell her? I was a teenager and being a teenager means, you are all grown up, right? Wrong!

Ever hear parents talking to their teens while saying, "I was young once too." Then you look at the teen who is unapologetically rolling their eyes, chewing their gum, and breathing deep sighs of annoyance, as if to say, "Really, Mom, really, Dad, were you???"
Back then we teens just thought we knew it all.

So, there I was on the train going to, "Far Rockaway," trying to act cool. Inwardly, I was working very hard to drown out the deafening, beating of my heart which was pounding louder and louder with each stop, which took me farther and farther away from home.

Oh yes, did I tell you about my seven o'clock curfew? Probably not, but my mom did not play when it came to keeping curfew. Shucks, you might even get locked out. So although I was trying to have fun,

I kept thinking about how long it was going to take to get back home. Thankfully, after a few hours we started heading back.

My friend's boyfriend and brother joined us for the ride.

They were a bunch of jokesters, and their laughter almost made me take my mind off of the clock, which seemed to be sprinting toward the seven o'clock hour.

Thankfully, we finally reached my stop, and I believe I had about seven minutes and not a moment to spare to get home. I was practically panicking, while trying to be cute at the same time. As we reached my stop, my friend, her boyfriend, and his brother decided they wanted to lollygag in the train station. So I left them.

I gave my goodbyes and dashed out of the train station and started racing for home, which was right around the corner, and then it happened...

There was a huge, gaping crack on the sidewalk, which I thought I could clear. Instead, my foot got caught in the crack, and I went crashing to the ground.

As I collided face forward with the pavement, my chest hit first and then my head snapped backwards. It was one of the scariest, most surreal experiences I have ever felt, because although I knew I had a body, after the fall, the only feeling I felt was from the midpoint of my neck upward. Everything else felt like air.

I felt no arms, no legs, no anything—just air. The only words I could get out as I gasped and tried to catch my breath was, "Oh God, Oh God!"

I want to pause here because I think it is important to mention, I was not religious or a consistent churchgoer. I was a Sinner. Around this time, I barely wanted to step foot in a church (I am not proud of this). As a matter of fact, I can remember telling one of my friends from school to put her Bible away when she was in my company.

Yet, in spite of my disobedience and lack of reverence for God, He knew I needed Him and extended His grace and mercy to me.

At this time my friends were still joshing around in the train station and had not come upstairs to help me, or to call 911.

It was just God and me. No one was there to pull me up or to tell me I was going to be okay. So, there I lay with my face to the pavement. I needed an intervention from on high.

Suddenly, I experienced a sensation in my back, which I can only describe as fingers going up and down my spine. As this sensation continued, the feeling was restored in my back, abdomen arms and legs, to the point where I was able to stand. For the life of me I could not understand why no one was walking up or down my side of the street that day.

As I stood up, too shaken to be embarrassed, I looked across the street and saw a man staring at me. He never said a word. He never came over to help. He was just looking. I was traumatized wondering, "What just happened to me?"

As I ran up the stairs to our brownstone, somehow I made it in time for curfew and went straight to my room.

That day I realized God heard me and saw me even before I fully came to know and love Him. It changed the trajectory of my thinking, so that when I hear people say, "God does not hear the Sinner," I beg to differ because of my personal experience.

I believe my Lord and Savior Jesus Christ recognizes the sincerity of the heart and humility of the soul more than the physical stance. I believe His purpose will be accomplished as we submit our lives to Him.

Do I ever feel pain in life? Absolutely! But I continue to believe in God. I learned there is someone bigger and greater than me who has all power. I now know sometimes He heals our physical body while other times He heals our emotions and sin-sick soul so that we are freed from the weight of sin, sadness, and pain.

We all go through various circumstances. Knowing God is with us makes all the difference in the world.

I believe we experience healing on different levels. There is healing of limbs, healing from broken hearts, healing from thoughts of inferiority, healing from sin, or healing from thoughts of defeat. It is healing that the thief on the cross received when he asked the Lord with an earnest heart to remember him when He went to His Kingdom.

This thief was fallen in his sins—he was a Sinner; he was a thief—but he knew enough to go to the one who knew how to pick him up and grant him salvation.

39One of the criminals hanging beside him scoffed, "So you're the Messiah, are you? Prove it by saving yourself-and us, too, while you're at it!"40But the other criminal protested, "Don't you fear God even when you have been sentenced to die? 41We deserve to die for our crimes, but this man hasn't done anything wrong."42Then he said, "Jesus, remember me when you come into your Kingdom."43And Jesus replied, "I assure you, today you will be with me in paradise. (Luke 23:39-43)

This was a man who had fallen, like me when I fell, who like me was not righteous by any means, yet he had an encounter with the Savior, the Lord Jesus Christ, the only begotten Son of God.

Because of the Love of God this thief was able to have life with the Lord beyond the grave.

I like many have prayed for loved ones to be healed and have not seen them receive healing. Yet, because of this scripture and many others like it, I take heart in knowing there is life after death, and God alone decides who is able to enter in.

I am so glad to know God is able to walk with us, touch us, comfort us, strengthen us, and pick us up from our fallen state. He wants us to call on Him, even if all we can get out is an "Oh God" or "Help me!"

When He calls for us to come forth in healing, to stand up in righteousness or to break through from depression, it will happen. Even if we have to ask more than once. Believe by faith and it can happen!

So with this I say, regardless of what state you find yourself in today, it does not matter if you have fallen, and if the entire world thinks there is no hope for you, the Almighty God has plans for your life.

He created you with purpose. He is hope for the hopeless, strength for the weary and healing for the broken.

It does not matter if your legs are too limp or too broken to physically stand, you can still rise in the midst of whatever circumstance you find yourself in.

Even if your faith is tiny—still believe. Do not be ashamed. Do not think you are unimportant or that God is too busy for you. Do not think your situation is too bleak. All you need is faith the size of a mustard seed (Matthew 17:20, NLT).

Reach out for God! Touch Him by faith. Look for Him through eyes of sincerity, with childlike faith. See God picking you up as you release your will and love to Him.

I see Him picking you up right now. I see Him dusting off the sadness and pain. I see you releasing your hurt and even forgiveness to Him. I see you finally letting go of anything that has kept you down.

It does not matter if you have experienced guilt, shame, grief, despondency or even rejection. Our Father knows and loves you more than anything.

It is time to stand up. God is your Maker. There is no need to hide or fear. He knows you, He loves you and He calls you His own. I pray you will always make the choice to rise up and know defeat is a state of mind and you do not need to accept it.

It is time to rise up. Let's keep going... Forward!

CHAPTER 13

BETWEEN HERE AND THERE

Today while standing in the kitchen an interesting thought came to mind, four simple words which piqued my interest and compelled me to reflect on them further, "Between here and there."

What is "Between here and there?" The middle, which often represents anticipation, frustration, exhilaration, hesitation, travail, and excitement. It's where the waiting happens.

One day I took a trip with my little one. As I packed our things, I was super excited. Finally, I thought, a moment to break away from the normalcy and repetition of everyday life. Praise God for new scenery. Hallelujah!

Yet, inclement weather and a malfunction with the defroster on the bus, caused a serious delay. Instead of arriving at nine o'clock, we arrived at eleven forty-five at night. Yikes!

My plan was to grab something to eat when my daughter and I reached the depot, but the delay ruined my well-thought-out plans. Thankfully we made it to one of the restaurants right before they closed. Yes! Score!

Either way, what I am trying to say is, "Have you ever had your well-defined plans go awry?"

When they do, discouragement and worry oftentimes try to settle in. It is a lot like receiving a prophecy stating things are going to get better and a new beginning is on the way with blessings and miracles. The only thing is, no one said how long one would have to wait before the vision became a reality.

Also, sooner or later we discover we cannot just sit and wait for the manifestation, we have to do something in the interim. Whether that something is writing out the vision, proclaiming it, looking for it, walking by faith, praying and praising until it happens, there is something we must do, even if it is believing and looking for the open door.

So you find yourself moving forward on a hope and promise. Poverty on one side, but promises of provision on the other; sickness in your body, but promises of healing on the other; unemployed, but believing you will move into the long awaited career or business you had been hoping for; told your marriage would be blessed, but just received papers to set the divorce in motion. My goodness—the waiting!

What do you do when you are between here and there; when you feel like holding on and giving up at the same time; when your smile almost resembles a smirk because you really don't feel like smiling in the first place?

In this space it hurts too much to laugh, and all you really want to do is cry. This can be a time where encouragement almost resembles noise, because you feel you have heard it all before and all you really want to know is when?

"Can somebody just give me the date of my deliverance and breakthrough here?" you might ask.

Yet, I have come to realize everything looks different when we look through the eyes of faith. I have accepted the only reason I have made it this far is because of the grace and mercy of God and the faith He allows me to have. Faith which has often literally been the *size of a mustard seed*

(Matthew 17:20). I literally went to the store and purchased a bottle of mustard seeds to remind me of God's promises when my faith was bleak.

I oftentimes think about the children of Israel and the moments they were discouraged.

Many times over, they were held captive by their enemy, sometimes because of just plain old attacks, other times due to disobedience, and other times just because it was part of the process.

Thankfully, as they continued to humble themselves and seek the God who does not fail, they were brought out of bondage time and time again. Sometimes through repentance. Other times through intentional consecration. What do you do when you are despondent and disappointment settles in? What do you do when everyone around you has given up and all you have is a promise? Hold on to the promise, seek the face of God for direction, and rejoice as your deliverance has already happened!

One day I asked myself this question, "Is God going to get anything out of this?"

I called it my "Job" experience and although I did not suffer to the magnitude he did, it was a very painful time. I ended up discovering the man I thought I would spend my eternity with was not forthcoming about his life. Actually he already had a life, one which I knew nothing about.

The marriage, his name, even the Reverend he used was fraudulent, and I was left to raise my daughter alone. I was broken beyond measure and wondered how something like this could have happened to me. I sent money for a home which I thought we would enjoy together, but one day he left for a long trip with his "job" (so I thought) and that was it.

I waited for many years thinking I was being a "good wife" not wanting to cause him any stress. I put my feelings to the side and encouraged him to be strong while we were apart. The birth of my daughter was difficult and called for an emergency C-section. I suffered a reaction from the epidural topper which sent pains spiking through my body. I felt lonely and abandoned. Thankfully two friends came to be with me. Thank you, Stephanie and Madelaine. Oh yes, and Nicole. Dan who was like family has gone on to be with the Lord, but I am grateful to him as well. That experience was craaaaaazzzzzzyyyyyyy! Okay, I had to get that out.

To add insult to injury, when I was scheduled to be discharged, the doctor told me she saw a hematoma and when she pulled it out she completely re-opened up my entire incision. All I felt was warmth trickling down my abdomen as she ran out of the room and came back with sheets to stop the bleeding. Sheesh!

What in the dickens was going on? *God, are you angry with me? God do you not love me anymore"* I thought I had done everything right, but if that was the case, why was this happening? I kept telling myself things were going to get better and I would have a blessed family, because I was told he and I would be together and things were going to be wonderful.

This was not the case. False prophesies and familiar spirits came into play. But especially, lies, lies, and more lies. I was being targeted, and it hurt like hell. These were some of the darkest days of my life.

There was no reasoning, I just knew things were going to get better. I had promises. I had prophesies. I had faith. But I have to add there are times when the enemy will use situations to try to break you, cause you to lose your mind, and even eventually destroy you. (See John 10:10; 1 Peter 5:8) It is not the person as much as it is the enemy behind the scenes pulling strings to bring you to nothing. Mercy—the Puppet Master pulling the strings. My gosh!

Earlier on, I had a gentleman making up horrible lies about me, but I was not aware of them because he caused me to believe he liked me. It turned out he seemed to have an ulterior motive. All I knew was people were looking at me so strangely, and I just did not know why.

This section is written as a testimony and to encourage someone, not to exploit. I realize so many people feel they have no voice and quietly suffer until their physical body is attacked from the intense weight of stress they are enduring. (Our bodies were not made to endure so much stress, and we must find ways to release it.) People feel alone, because their story seems so strange, so crazy, so much like a movie, until they just suffer alone.

I thought the same thing about my circumstance, but I now know I am not the only one who has gone through many of the things I have encountered.

Mostly, I have come to know God causes us to give voice to the voiceless! Come on Deborah's arise! The main reason for writing this is to let someone know they are not alone and the situation they have gone through is not isolated and crazy.

Also, if you have heard something negative about a person, it is important to seek the Lord and pray for both individuals, because sometimes what you may be told is not true at all. Seek the truth.

It is important that those of us who are spiritual learn to restore the broken with humility.

For me, it was not until years later when I heard about some of the rumors. I was shocked and just could not lead myself to believe it. *Why would he do something like this?* I helped him with various accomplishments I cooked for him. I encouraged him. Why? Then the thought came to me, *if a man or woman can only celebrate you behind closed doors, but can humiliate you in public after calling you a term of endearment in private, seek the Lord, and nine times out of ten, run!*

Run like there are jet engines on your shoes, and run for your life— at least that is what I told myself after the fact. I can laugh at this now, but back then, I cried long and hard because I hate wasting time. I do not like pouring my affection into empty spaces with holes. The Word of the Lord tells us to *Guard our heart.* –(Proverbs 4:23)

So I had to pray long and hard so I could forgive myself for not seeing the signs, and then I had to forgive individuals for allowing the enemy to use them or just for plain old immaturity. Everything is not the enemy. Who knows, maybe they were not even aware or perhaps they just did not care, but that is not for me to try to figure out. Through it all, God kept letting me know He knew me more than anyone else. He let me know he saw everything that transpired and that He loved me, despite what people said, thought, or did.

I realized God could get the glory out of every experience. Through it all, I accepted I did not have to spend my time trying to please people, I only had to love them as God commands.

Yes, I had to forgive t hose who hurt me and release the offenses to God, holding on to them would only prevent me from moving forward.

Yes between here and there was God!

He never left me. He never forsook me. He never told me I was not good enough, beautiful enough, or smart enough.

He was present, and He had certain people like my friends, Tony and Alisa Barnes, who were in a different state, but who kept praying for me and encouraging me through it all.

He used people who were strangers like Ms. Bryant, Ms. Brown, Ms. Vera, and Ms. Phyllis, who saw what I could not see. I wondered how they could call me "Woman of God" when all of those horrible things had happened to me, and I felt so discouraged. Yet, I still cried out to God and found ways to give Him thanks in spite of the discouragement.

Did Jesus Christ stop being King when he was homeless and born in a manger instead of a palace?

Did Christ lose his power when he was spat on, lied about, and called everything but the Son of the living God? Was He no longer loved, because He was brutally beaten and crucified on a cross with thieves and sinners?

No, and although I had not suffered to that magnitude, I realized God loved me just as much when I was on the mountain as when I was in the valley. God had a purpose for it all and that He was going to bring me through all of the mixed up emotions, rejection, character assassination, and loss with victory.

The greatest songs are often penned in the depths of adversity. My responsibility was to accept it happened, release my disappointment and trust God as I moved ahead. I had to change my focus from the problem to the Problem Solver; from the heartache to the Mender of the Wounded Heart; from the struggle, to the One who made rivers in the desert, and from lack and poverty to the Provider who gave manna from Heaven.

He became my all and all. He became the true source of my joy. He gave me the courage to forge ahead despite everything I saw and felt. I was able to say, "God is our refuge and strength, always ready to help in times of trouble. So we will not fear when earthquakes come and the mountains crumble into the sea." (Psalm 46:1-2)

Instead of rehearsing the problem, I started to focus on the promises of God. I took my mind off of those who I felt failed me and thought more and more about the love of God.

So although between here and there, it felt like the floor was being pulled from underneath me, I learned to reach up and grab hold of God through faith. I quoted the promises of God rather than rehearsed the lies of the enemy.

If you are between here and there, have faith! Remember God's promises.

Get real, real close to God. Press towards your purpose and know God is with you in whatever state you may find yourself. Keep moving forward...

CHAPTER 14

THE RESILIENT

There are some who will hate to see you rise after they've watched you fall Get up anyway! Some who despise the sound of your voice and your message - Speak it anyway!

There are those who are grateful that the sweet melody of your song has been silenced – Sing it anyway!

Some who have voiced, they wish you were dead, ignore it and live anyway! Some who make you feel as if there is nothing to your praise Go ahead you are a winner – shout it and dance anyway!

As I come to the final chapter of this manuscript, I can imagine a group of men, women, boys and girls cheering while calling out your name and shouting from the rafters, while banging on the bleachers saying, "Don't Give Up! Don't Give Up! Don't Give Up!"

I can picture some of us on large movie screens, living life, while going through difficult obstacles and triumphs. Sometimes crying, sometimes laughing, sometime singing and sometimes dancing.

I can envision those who are watching us laughing with glee as they observe us persevere through discouragement and trials. I believe these are the great cloud of witnesses, those who have gone on before us who are cheering us on.

The screen then changes and I visualize another group of people who appear to be waiting, while clutching and wringing their hands. Many of them have tears in their eyes and appear to be frustrated and ready to give up. I soon realize these are the ones who are waiting for your testimony and my testimony.

They are longing to hear a narrative which demonstrates how you and I received grace and strength to forge ahead, despite unsurmountable odds. A story which tells how we found the ability to dream, to hope and to live again after we experienced intense pain.

"Ahaaa!" I say, as I slap my thigh, while rocking back and forth and shaking my head up and down, "So this is what it is all about!" One way or another, God uses everything—the good, what seems bad, the annoying, and even the frustrating—to bring Him glory. Somehow in the midst of it all, He creates ways to strengthen us, stretch us and teach us of His abounding, unselfish love and promise.

It is in the middle of here on the way to there, while trusting God's power over ours, we confront our insecurities, find our motivation, and move toward our mission and purpose in life.

I imagined dreams being dusted off, dances being expressed, books being written, songs being sung, love being shared, and purpose being fulfilled as people started to embrace individuality and accept and operate in their God-given gifts and talents.

Your gift was never made to settle inside of you. Talents and gifts do not serve much purpose when they are not being used. Have you used your gift lately or has it been stifled as you spend time focusing on those who do not think you have a voice or anything to say to begin with?

Breaking News! Your voice and life was never made to be silenced or to appease others.

It is true not everyone will preach on pulpits or stand before millions, but everyone has a purpose and everyone has a voice. Perhaps your purpose can be found in your prayer room, in your family, on your job, in your business or ministry and life at large.

So if your audible voice is the vehicle used to bring about change, use it even if it cracks and shakes from years of being dormant and stifled. Even if your pronunciation is imperfect and you are not grammatically sound, use it anyway. Your message can additionally be articulated through art, dance, writing, in advocacy, or initiatives, in helping or serving the disenfranchised, but mainly it must be expressed.

At this moment I wonder about your days and nights and pray they are filled with comfort, companionship, and community. I hope you have developed a loving relationship with the Almighty God who sees, knows, and loves you greatly. I wonder if you realize His presence is all around you, even now. He speaks to you through various means. I pray you are able to see, hear, and soak in His presence while recognizing His voice.

I hope you are able to accept your challenges are not just a vehicle to make you strong, but they can also be used to show you the power which resides inside of you and mostly the power of the Almighty God.

There is a strength that is magnified in weakness-(2 Corinthians 12:9). I want you to grab hold of this concept and celebrate in knowing your struggles were never created to destroy you. Truly, the grace of God has carried you this far!

Just knowing you have made it to this chapter of life is additionally a testimony to your bravery.

I wonder if you are someone who has resorted to wrestling with private struggles behind closed doors, sometimes in complete silence, hoping and praying that someone—anyone—would see your complications and discern your inner cries.

May God send the right people into your life to comfort you and may you be able to accept their love, support, and encouragement when they come.

I pray that children will sleep peacefully through the night as their caregivers are rejuvenated. May you realize, today and right now, you are enough and as you live and grow with the help of God you will be enough for every tomorrow.

You see, I discovered how important God is and without Him, my efforts are futile. The level of empathy you receive for others after having gone through turmoil is worth it all.

As I write I recalled those who I saw on public transportation who were no longer able to fight back their tears, who cried in the midst of strangers. I did too.

I thought of the broken-hearted, the silent sufferers, pastors, pastor's wives, teachers, preachers, business owners, male, female, children, and parents who felt alone and defeated.

I thought of those who wept alone and then gained enough strength to make it through the day and then resorted back to a place of despondency.

How I wish I could shout from the rooftop—DON' T GIVE UP!

The God of all comfort, promises to be with you and to walk with you through the valley. You see, I struggled in writing this last chapter because I wanted to write a happy ending with a symphonic closure filled with harmonious crescendos and cataclysmic, awe-inspiring paragraphs filled with positivity and bliss.

Yet, I realize many have been led to believe there must always be happiness all around. Truthfully, I do not think anyone likes to see happy endings more than me. But I realize this type of thinking can become a smoke screen which obstructs the truth and reality of life. The reality is God's peace is able to strengthen us even through moments of turmoil. Yes, His grace is sufficient.

So, I focus on the truth, a truth which is literal and practical, which merely states in whatever space I find myself, the Almighty God is able to sustain and give grace and guidance. The truth is He created us with emotions and those emotions allow us to be human. We will cry and we will laugh. We will mourn and we will dance.

Ecclesiastes 3:1-10 put it best, [1]For everything there is a season, a time for every activity under heaven. [2]A time to be born and a time to die. A time to plant and a time to harvest. [3]A time to kill and a time to heal. A time to tear down and a time to build up. [4]A time to cry and a time laugh. A time to grieve and a time to dance.

[5]A time to scatter stones and a time to gather stones. A time to embrace and a time to turn away. [6]A time to search and a time to quit searching. A time to keep and a time to throw away. [7]A time to tear and a time to mend. A time to be quiet and a time to speak. [8]A time to love and a time to hate. A time for war and a time for peace.

The aforementioned scripture speaks of the significance of understanding and accepting there are times and seasons for every purpose under heaven.

I think this scripture gives us permission to accept our emotions and to know it is okay to express them in a way that does not discredit the future.

There is a season for everything and God is with us in every season.

Many times the temperature of the trial can sometimes cause us to lose sight, especially when there is trouble all around.

You may feel stuck today because of the devastation you have encountered, yet I pray your mind will be released from the spirit of offense, anxiety and turmoil, and if you are stuck, I pray you be set free.

Your present circumstance can change in an instant. So always remember your current status and situation does not define you. It is God who defines you! It is never "what" that defines us. Not our money, not our job, not our homes because those things come and go. But the faithfulness of God always remains.

Perhaps, you have experienced physical changes. Please do not let this be a barrier to inner determination. Let the buoyancy of your inner strength and Holy Spirit allow you to rise, even if you can no longer physically stand. Let the strength of your voice and your determined soul be heard.

This is exactly what having "Snapbacktivity" means.; it is more than a state of being, but a will and intent to forge ahead despite obstacles, enemies, and failures.

It is more than a positive thought alone; it is also an action to do, to be, to advance, and to become. It is the acceptance and acknowledgement of a problem, coupled by the determination to find the solution.

It is realizing we all have a positive purpose and voice which cannot be silenced by years of rejection and complexity. It is acknowledging the importance of conversing with God like

"Grandma Wisdom," who allowed her prayer life to be the catalyst which changed the trajectory of her broken-hearted granddaughter while giving her a reason to smile. Yes, thank God for the "Grandma Wisdoms" of the world and their "hook up to Heaven."

Your message can be shared through your talent, your publication, your speech, your advocacy for the less fortunate, your articulation for the voice-less and unheard. These are all a means of embracing, owning, and walking in the power of resilience. Come on now, speak it!

It is the moment where you realized you were in the midst of a great struggle, but somehow found the strength to go through it and persevere, despite the lack of support you may have encountered.

It is feeling the beat of your own heart, urging you to move forward and causing you to live, despite the inner struggle which keeps telling you to stop.

It is the tenacity of those who have been "Duped," who find a way to open the blinds and let the light and love in again. It is about those who identify with the pliability of the butterfly in "Butterfly Wings," who was still able to spread its wings and fly, even after experiencing severe tragic moments that threatened its existence and ability to emerge from a chrysalis that no longer had the capacity to contain it.

It is the story of those who said, "I can't swim," or wondered, "Does Foster care?" It is about those who were "Duped" and bullied but one day found out they had more potential and a reason to live far beyond their wildest dreams and imagination. They found their voice amidst the struggle.

It is the story of single mothers and fathers and those who mourned the loss of loved ones or those who became caregivers while shedding tears in silence over the kitchen sink. Yes, it was hard and may still be hard, but you have and will continue to survive and even thrive!

God loves me! God loves you! Despite what the enemy may want you to believe. It is not God who often brings the storms, but it is God who walks with us through the storms.

Our Sustainer, Provider, Shelter, Regulator, and Friend! He has given us the ability to persevere through it all. When one door closes, look for another, but don't give up. When people abandon you, don't give up!

When the money is funny, don't give up! When you are alone, don't give up! When you are celebrated by many, don't give up!

When you believe, don't give up, and when you can't find the strength to believe, don't give up.

You may be in a shelter, but let me help you—Jesus was born in a manger and is still the King of Kings. Don't give up! It's only temporary.

Don't give up on your present! Don't give up on your future! Don't give up on your purpose! Don't give up on your family! Don't give up on yourself! Don't give up on your children! Don't give up on your parents! Don't give up on your business! Don't give up on your employees! Don't give up on your life!

Don't give up on the promises of God which go beyond the here and now; to a place where there are no more tears, no more lies, and no more goodbyes!

Don't give up on your destiny! Don't give up on the One who created you for a purpose!

Even when the tears fall, don't give up! Even when you feel alone, don't give up!

Even when you have failed – Don't give up! Even when they turn their backs on you – don't give up.

When they love you – don't give up and when they don't love you - don't give up! When you have been used and abused – don't you give up! When they hear you and don't listen – don't give up! Even when there appears to be death and sorrow all around – please don't give up!

Your future depends on you pushing ahead. Your unlived God-given dreams and purpose all need to become a reality! So believe in yourself, and mostly believe in the God who created you to be uniquely you.

Embrace your individuality in Christ. Celebrate your existence and allow God to take you to the highest of heights! I truly believe He has wonderful things in store for you.

Always remember you are loved and have purpose.

Rejoice and live! Trust God for greater! Be thankful for where you have been, where you are, and for where you are going! Your future is in the Almighty God's capable hands.

I am decreeing freedom, breakthrough, and advancement over your life!

Breathe, love, and shine. Never be afraid of having big dreams or of breaking out of the mold that may have tried to captivate your thoughts while holding you hostage. It's time to increase and advance by faith. You can do this! You have to do this! You were born to succeed.

Trust God with your life and plans. If you fail, try again. Someone is waiting for your story and testimony. Keep moving forward. You are royalty. You are brave, and you can make it. Here's to better days ahead.

Claim your inheritance, walk in victory, serve the Lord in love, and whatever you do—don't give up!

Don't Give Up!

Jesus does love you. If you do not know Christ as your personal Lord and Savior, or if you feel the need to be renewed; Repent and ask the Lord for forgiveness in faith; not condemnation, shame or guilt. Repentance keeps the lines of communication open with God and humanity. Repentance if not only feeling sorry for sins, but also making the choice to turn away from them. God has called you to love Him with your whole heart, mind, body and soul.

I make repentance a daily practice and repent as soon as I even think something wrong. I also ask for forgiveness for things I don't know about. It helps to incorporate this practice every day.

Ask the Lord to come into your heart and to reveal His love and purpose.

Remember your tomorrow can look totally different from your today, so don't lose hope.

Find a faith-filled, compassionate group of Believers to do life with. We were not made to figure out life alone.

Everyday choose to walk in victory and not defeat.

"Seek help when you need it, cry when you must and celebrate yourself and others often."

Like to leave a review on Amazon. Here's the link:
amazon.com/author/yedidahspann

Website: yedidahspann.com or iamyedidahspann.com

Listen to Pep Talk with Yedidah on Spreaker, iHeartRadio and Apple Podcasts.